THE FIRST
CAMBRIDGE PRESS IN ITS
EUROPEAN SETTING

PLATE I

Bullock's copy of Gaza's *Greek Grammar* (see Appendix A, p. 70, no. 20)

THE FIRST
CAMBRIDGE PRESS IN ITS
EUROPEAN SETTING

BY

E. P. GOLDSCHMIDT

THE SANDARS LECTURES IN
BIBLIOGRAPHY, 1953

CAMBRIDGE
AT THE UNIVERSITY PRESS
1955

CAMBRIDGE UNIVERSITY PRESS
Cambridge, New York, Melbourne, Madrid, Cape Town, Singapore,
São Paulo, Delhi, Dubai, Tokyo

Cambridge University Press
The Edinburgh Building, Cambridge CB2 8RU, UK

Published in the United States of America by Cambridge University Press, New York

www.cambridge.org
Information on this title: www.cambridge.org/9780521143325

© Cambridge University Press 1955

First published 1955
This digitally printed version 2010

A catalogue record for this publication is available from the British Library

ISBN 978-0-521-05108-8 Hardback
ISBN 978-0-521-14332-5 Paperback

CONTENTS

ILLUSTRATIONS

FOREWORD

E. P. GOLDSCHMIDT was a bookseller who was much more interested in reading and studying the books he sold than in the actual profit he made from their sale. His interest in books started in his early Cambridge days, 1905–9, and until the end of the twenties it was mainly concentrated on incunabula, bookbindings and medieval authors. His researches in early printing will be found spread through the *Gesamtkatalog der Wiegendrucke*. His interest in bookbindings produced his first large work, *Gothic and Renaissance Bookbindings* (London, Benn, 1928), still one of the standard works on the subject.

During the last thirty years he became more and more interested in humanists, the printing of their books, and the gradual spread of their ideas and influence throughout the continent of Europe. References to Erasmus and his circle, and Lucian of Samosata and his influence on the humanists, will be found on almost every one of the following pages.

Mediaeval Texts and their first Appearance in Print (his favourite work) was published by the Bibliographical Society in 1943. Three lectures on type, ornament and illustration, given at a number of Institutions in the U.S.A. and in this country, were published by the Cambridge University Press in 1950 under the title, *The Printed Book of the Renaissance*.

When in May 1952 he was elected Sandars Reader in Bibliography for 1953, he set aside all other work and gathered together his many notes on the history of humanism and printing after 1500. Unfortunately his health was already bad, and it soon became clear that he would be unable to deliver the lectures in person. It was, in fact, uncertain whether he would be able to complete them at all. With great determination, however, he refused to give in to his increasing physical weakness, and passed and corrected the final proofs of the text three days before his death last February. Had he been in better health and with more time at his disposal, it is probable that he would have made a number of enlargements and changes. It was decided, however, to publish the work as he left it, as a useful basis for the further study of this interesting period in European history, and I have had the satisfaction of seeing his proofs through to publication.

FOREWORD

The author was indebted to a large number of people, and, as usual, it is impossible to mention them all. Special thanks however are due to H. R. Creswick, Cambridge University Librarian, who encouraged and helped in the publication of this book, and supplied much help and information on many occasions; and to the many friends at the University Press, who were always most helpful, and many times showed almost angelic patience and understanding. Miss Phyllis Giles most kindly prepared the index.

To them, and all his other friends and helpers, this work is gratefully dedicated.

J. L. VELLEKOOP

LONDON
Autumn 1954

PREFACE

FOR THESE LECTURES I have wilfully chosen a subject, the First Cambridge Press, on which, you might think, all that is needed has been said by scholars as eminent as Henry Bradshaw, George Gray, Gordon Duff, and my immediate teacher in matters of early printing, Francis Jenkinson.*

I do not, however, propose to discuss Siberch's press on the same lines on which these illustrious predecessors have dealt with it. They have assembled the output of the press, located the extant copies and analysed its typographic equipment. I have no new discoveries to announce, such as the *Prognostication* which F. S. Ferguson published in the first volume of *Transactions of the Cambridge Bibliographical Society*, thereby adding not only a new title but also a new type to Siberch's canon; or Mr D. M. Rogers' find of an Indulgence in the same new type communicated in the *Bodleian Library Record* of December 1952.

What I wish to speak about might be described as the literary characteristics of the publishing venture of Siberch and his scholarly backers. Seen in isolation, the short-lived Cambridge typographical experiment of 1521–2 may appear as a freakish, somewhat inexplicable, enterprise, foredoomed to prompt failure. Of the ten titles chosen for publication the preponderant majority were of such a limited appeal that, viewed as a business undertaking, Siberch's press could hardly hope to prosper.

It is necessary, I would suggest, to survey a wider field, to consider Siberch's activity in comparison with similar enterprises in other university towns on the Continent, to recognise it as the symptomatic utterance of a compelling and universal European movement, if we would try to understand the reason for its occurrence.

If this is the task I have rashly undertaken it is a very big one. I must at the outset, I fear, beg your indulgence for giving but a sketchy and very imperfect account of a vast subject, which would require years of single-minded labour to present authoritatively and with sufficient first-hand knowledge of the relevant facts.

* The notes are at p. 57.

ix

In order to draw comparisons with continental analogies it is unavoidable first to give some account of the books Siberch chose to print. Therefore the first of my three lectures will be devoted to a descriptive enumeration of the ten books Siberch completed during his short career. In my second lecture I will try to sketch the situation and the attitude of the humanist enthusiasts in the European universities about 1520, and especially the emphasis then given to Greek studies. The third of my lectures will deal with the printing offices in the University towns which placed themselves at the disposal of the humanist authors. The striking resemblances of their equipment, their output and all too frequently, their sorry fate, will I hope, illuminate a promising though short-lived movement in European letters.

E. P. G.

January 1954

I

SIBERCH'S TEN BOOKS

JOHN LAER of Siegburg, near Cologne, who generally, but not always, called himself John Siberch in Cambridge, must have had some useful acquaintances in this university before he came to settle here as a printer and bookbinder. Presumably he was acting as an agent for Cologne and Antwerp booksellers, travelling to and fro, visiting his English customers, and incidentally carrying letters as he did so. The earliest mention of him is in a letter from Erasmus in April 1518, from which we learn that Siberch called on him at Louvain without bringing a letter from Jo. Caesarius of Cologne.* His business at that time would be analogous to that of John Dorn of Brunswick, whose 'Daybook' as an Oxford bookseller covering the year 1520 was published by F. Madan in 1885. That Siberch, apart from the brief interlude of his experiment in printing, was active as a bookseller and bookbinder while at Cambridge can be gathered from the letter by Peter Kaetz to him, which Gordon Duff discovered in one of his bindings.*

In May 1520 Siberch, while still connected with the Cologne book trade, commissioned and financed the printing of the *Introductiones ad Rudimenta Graeca* by Richard Croke of Eton and King's* from the press of Eucharius Cervicornus at Cologne. This was but a reprint of a Leipzig edition from the press of Valentin Schumann entitled *Tabulae Graecas Literas Discere Cupientibus Utiles*, which Croke had issued there while teaching Greek in Leipzig University from 1514 to 1517 (Proctor 11512). Croke had learnt his Greek from William Grocyn at London,* from Erasmus at Cambridge and from Jerome Aleander at Paris.* He stayed in Paris for some time (1511–13), and while there he saw the first edition of Erasmus' *Encomium Moriae* through the press* of Gilles de Gourmont, with whom he established a close friendship, becoming the godfather of one of his sons.* From Paris he went on to Louvain, Cologne and Leipzig. He concludes a dedicatory letter of an edition of Ausonius, printed at Leipzig by Schumann in 1515, with the words: 'Vale, et Crocum tuum primum literarum Graecarum Colonie Lovanii Lypsieque publicum professorem ama.'*

In 1518 Croke returned to Cambridge, having been appointed to the Greek readership, an honour on which Erasmus congratulated him in a letter of April 1518 (Ep. 827), and of which he declared himself to be unworthy in a speech in praise of Greek studies held in July 1519.* For his Greek course Croke needed an elementary text-book for his students, and he commissioned Siberch to have his *Rudimenta* printed for him by someone possessing Greek type. It would seem that Siberch carried the copies with him when he came to Cambridge in the same year,* and that he also brought back Croke's original manuscript. A fragment of it was discovered by Gordon Duff in a book bound by Siberch now in the Westminster Abbey Library, and is reproduced in G. J. Gray's *Cambridge Stationers*, Plate XXV.

Through Croke no doubt, if he had not met them before as a travelling bookseller, Siberch came to know other important members of the University who were interested in philological studies. Men of very great influence, for they achieved something quite astonishing on his behalf. Some time between Michaelmas 1520 and Michaelmas 1521 they obtained a loan of £20 for him from the University funds, no doubt to help him set up his press. That this advance was never repaid and was carried in the University books as owing, down to 1553, is not for our purposes of material importance, though it does not speak well for the credit of Siberch or of his guarantors, or for the efficiency of the administration of the University finances.*

Siberch's bond was guaranteed by four resident members. They were Robert Ridley (D.D. 1518), uncle of Nicholas Ridley, bishop of London, and Robert Wakefield (B.A. 1514), the Hebrew scholar who had returned from teaching at the Collegium Trilingue at Louvain in 1519 and was then incorporated M.A.* The third guarantor is an otherwise unknown 'Dr Maundefelde'. The fourth, Henry Bullock of Queens' College (D.D. 1520) became Siberch's most active patron and the author of two of his ten books.*

By February 1521 Siberch's press was in working order and its first product was Henry Bullock's speech of welcome to Cardinal Wolsey when he came on a visit to Cambridge in autumn 1520. It is a small quarto of eight leaves, a fine Latin oration, composed by a financial backer of the press and in praise of a powerful patron of university studies. That is a typical beginning for a printing press started in a university town in furtherance of humanist aims, of 'bonae literae', of eloquence and of stylistic elegance.

We are reminded of the first of all academic presses founded in 1470 in the most ancient of universities, in Paris. Just as Croke and Bullock brought Siberch from Cologne to print in Cambridge, so two masters of Paris, John Heynlin of Stein and Guillaume Fichet, called three printers from Basle and set them to work within the precincts of the Collège de la Sorbonne. Heynlin had himself studied at Basle and seen the printers there at work. He it was who called the craftsmen; Fichet, an ardent enthusiast for the humanist New Learning, provided the money for starting the enterprise. The Sorbonne press did not last much longer than Siberch's Cambridge venture: three years. And among the first books they printed was Fichet's own *Rhetorica*.

Bullock's *Oratio*, Fichet's *Rhetorica*, and the analogous foreign examples I will cite later on, let us perceive one of the motives which led the humanist scholars to demand the services of a printing press, and to be willing even to make financial sacrifices in order to see themselves in print. If we are unkind we will call it vanity and a desire for self-advertisement. It is not wholly fair, however, to describe their thirst for printer's ink in such simple terms. The theologian—or rather the priest—, the lawyer, the physician had many recognised avenues by which he could further his career, without having to demonstrate his capacity for original composition. The 'man of letters', the scholar whose aim was a perfect command of elegant and persuasive language, had to make his attainments known by a wide distribution of his writings. Whether he hoped for employment at the court or in diplomacy, or whether he thought of advancement in university or other teaching appointments, he had to bring samples of his style to the notice of as many potential patrons as possible. Before the invention of printing we find the humanists dedicating and re-dedicating their efforts to a multiplicity of princes, bishops and other influential magnates. Envisaged in terms of actual, concrete, books this implies a copying and re-copying of the work he was offering every time some contact with a likely patron made such a labour seem worth while. From extant dedication manuscripts of Fichet's *Rhetorica* we can estimate to what heavy expenditure on vellum, calligraphers and miniaturists an author who could afford to do so might go in order to submit his book to a succession of useful patrons. It is to these seekers after employment that the invention of printing must have appeared not only as a time-saving blessing but as a substantial economy.

The recording in print of elegant speeches made on ceremonial occasions soon became an established practice for bringing a scholar's oratorical attainments to the notice of competent judges or prospective supporters. Another recognised method for gaining a reputation for learning was to display a knowledge of Greek by publishing a Latin translation of a choice and unknown Greek text.

Bullock's second book, issued by Siberch soon after the *Oratio*, is his version of Lucian's Περὶ διψάδων, a short piece of only five pages. The subject is a strange one. The Dipsades, as you probably all know, are a species of venomous snake existing in the deserts of Libya, whose bite causes an unquenchable raging thirst which ends in speedy death. In the last paragraph Lucian turns his medico-zoological disquisition into a parable, likening himself to the victim bitten by love for the audience he is addressing, and insatiable in his desire for their company. Only when we reach that forced twist do we realise that this piece is not intended as a factual account of the dangerous fauna in the Sahara desert, but is just another rhetorical exercise of the Syrian satirist, a model 'exordium' for some fine speech. It certainly is one of his least successful efforts.

Still, it had never yet been translated from the Greek. (There were by 1521 two complete Greek editions of Lucian's works: Florence, 1496 and Venice, 1503.) It was but little known, it was short and it was easy. It could be offered as a presentable specimen of Greek erudition. So Bullock dedicated his version to Nicholas West, bishop of Ely, one of Henry VIII's prelate-diplomats. He added at the end a reprint of his *Oratio* to Wolsey and a complimentary letter he had received about it. On the last page, above the colophon, he inserted four short Greek maxims with their interlinear Latin translations. Either these or the two Greek words on the title of the St Augustine are the first appearance of any Greek type in England.

Bullock's endeavour to demonstrate his talents did help him to attain his object: he was soon appointed one of Cardinal Wolsey's chaplains. No doubt he also believed that the publication of his compositions through the printing press had for all time secured his fame as an author, and, in a strictly bibliographical sense, it has done so. The writer of the first book printed at Cambridge is assured that his name will never disappear from typographical gazetteers. If, however, Henry Bullock as a scholar is not entirely forgotten, that is due not to his compositions but to his close association with Erasmus of Rotterdam. From their correspondence it becomes evident that Bullock (or Bovillus, as Erasmus called him) was in contact with Erasmus while he was working on his Greek New Testament in Cambridge (August 1511–January 1514); he undoubtedly was one of his Greek pupils. But foremost of all, Bullock's reputation rests on the lengthy letter (Ep. 456) which Erasmus addressed to him from Rochester in August 1516.

Erasmus' New Testament had come out at Basle in February of that year and it contains among the preliminaries after the dedication to Pope Leo X, an 'Apologia' seeking to justify the bold undertaking. It could be foreseen that it was likely to cause a storm of protest among the less progressive theologians. On its appearance the expected attacks soon did materialise with some violence; in this letter itself we learn that at one Cambridge college the Fellows had solemnly forbidden any copies of the dangerous volume to enter the college precincts. Erasmus' letter to Bullock is in the main an extension and amplification of the 'Apologia'. To the more general arguments advanced in the 'Apologia' as printed in the Basle New Testament, Erasmus now adds more specific rejoinders to attacks that had actually been made and come to his knowledge in the intervening months. The letter was published by Erasmus himself in January 1518 in one of the earliest collections of his own letters which he saw through the press, printed by Froben at Basle.* It was of course incorporated in all the subsequent editions of Erasmus' *Correspondence* and *Collected Works*. It is this momentous epistle which has carried Bullock's name down the centuries and will for all time lead its readers to ask the question: Who was the Henricus Bovillus to whom it is addressed?

Henry Bullock, after being Vice-Chancellor in 1524–5, died in 1526. The books he possessed were taken over by Queens' College and a list of their titles is preserved in the college archives. It is a characteristic library of a humanist, containing a number of Greek authors in their recent Aldine editions. We give the list with comments in Appendix A, p. 69.

From Siberch's press we have one volume by Erasmus himself, but it can hardly be regarded as contributing to the glory of Cambridge. The *Libellus de Conscribendis Epistolis*, a quarto of eighty leaves published in

October 1521, is quite indisputably a first edition, as it proudly announces on the title: 'Nunc primum prodit in lucem.' The further descriptive qualifications on the title-page: 'A work long ago begun by him in a sketchy manner, then taken up again for refurbishing but interrupted' are also quite truthful—in a way. But perhaps it would have been better to ask Erasmus' permission.

What Erasmus thought of this unsolicited and unauthorised offering we learn with some force from the prefatory letter addressed to Nicolas Bérauld, which he printed in front of an entirely remodelled and rewritten 'genuine' edition issued from Froben's press a few months later in August 1522.* 'Since that man Holonius has ceased to be among the living', it begins—Holonius was the culprit responsible for supplying a garbled and interpolated manuscript of Erasmus' *Colloquia* to a printer without Erasmus' knowledge—

Since that man Holonius has ceased to be among the living, I really thought I no longer had to fear that someone else might make public some childishness which as a youngster I had written to exercise my pen or to comply with the wishes of some friends, never thinking of publishing it. And, would you believe it, quite suddenly there arises in England another Holonius who prints my book *De Componendis Epistolis* which I began to write in Paris nearly thirty years ago for an untrustworthy friend, a fitting present for such a character. On its preparation and composition I spent no more than twenty days; and so little did I then care to finish the book, that I gave him my original draft to carry away with him (for he was just about to go on a long journey) without keeping a copy for myself. Some time later, some friends who, I don't know how, had got hold of these scribbles and had taken copies of them, begged me that I should work out these rudiments of a book; for it was nothing but a rough draft and also incomplete and defective. I took it in hand, but when I began to re-write it, I liked it less than ever and threw the whole thing away. Never did it enter my head that somebody might be so impudent as to publish my notes, at least as long as I was alive and able to protest. But truly, as I begin to see now, there is nothing a printer would be ashamed to do. Once they have found out that nothing sells better than the most worthless rubbish, while the classical and proven authors are neglected, the printers with a brazen face follow the satyrist's maxim: Money smells good whatever it is made of.*

The faithless friend, the 'amicus parum sincerus', for whom Erasmus wrote the treatise on letter-writing, was Robert Fisher,* a kinsman of John Fisher, bishop of Rochester. Erasmus presented him with it in Paris in the spring of 1498, just before Robert Fisher left for Italy. He died young at an unknown date, but before 1511, so that he cannot be held responsible for Siberch's publication. Siberch's manuscript, whoever supplied him with the copy, did however contain the dedicatory letter to Fisher with which Erasmus accompanied his gift and which is printed in front of the Cambridge edition. P. S. Allen does not doubt its authenticity and includes it in *Op. Ep.* (I, no. 71), with one of his admirable introductory notes. It contains little of substance but it has a passage ('Quid enim critici dicent, imo quid non dicent, ubi viderint ausum me tractare rem a tam multis, tam eruditis scriptoribus scite diligenterque tractatam') which, if genuine, clearly gives the lie to Erasmus' disclaimers of any intention to publish. On the other hand Allen's exact investigations have established that the Cambridge text contains passages referring to events later than Robert Fisher's departure for Italy. Whether these were inserted by a copyist, or perhaps by Erasmus himself when he was refurbishing the book in Cambridge in 1511, must remain an open question.*

But what was in the mind of Siberch and his backers and abettors when they embarked on this unfortunate venture? Did they genuinely believe they were laying a welcome tribute at the famous Erasmus' feet by publishing his old treatise on the art of letter-writing? Did they omit to ask his permission merely because they would not spoil the surprise of presenting him with a long-forgotten work of his own?

Not a bit of it. They very clearly foresaw what was coming. Siberch the printer himself prefixes to his book a lengthy letter of dedication to Bishop John Fisher, who was then Chancellor of Cambridge University. It is so curious that I hope you will forgive me for reading a good deal of it to you.

A short time ago a friend of mine brought me this book. He said that he himself, years since, had copied it from Erasmus' autograph and he asked me to print it. He tried to persuade me that there was no better way for me to gain Erasmus' friendship than by doing so. Not only would I not wish to offend that eminent man in the slightest matter, there never was anything dearer to my heart's desire than that I might some day find an opportunity of doing something agreeable to Erasmus. I must sincerely confess to Your Lordship that I could hardly be induced to undertake the task, even by such a close friend and a man of great learning; and that for many reasons but especially because I know only too well what a nasty response a man from the Netherlands* got for a very similar enterprise. I mean him who published his Colloquia under Erasmus' name without first consulting him. So unless You yourself in such a dilemma had intervened unexpectedly like a power from above, it could hardly have come about that this little book printed with my own types could have seen the light....you are all-powerful with Erasmus....I confidently expected that this book if it were offered from your Lordship's hands to your British countrymen and also abroad, would not only be received everywhere with open arms, but that even Erasmus might bear with my boldness. That he might not be angry with me, though he may not approve of what I did, and that he might, as he has done in other cases, if he finds any faults in it, for the sake of Your favour put the last polish on the book which up till now has been so long and so anxiously awaited....You would hardly believe how much everybody applauded me when the rumours of this book first got about. Nor is it easy to give you an idea how they clamoured for it from day to day. When I had at last finished it it is incredible how they hurried along to embrace me, how eagerly they bought it up, and how they kissed the copies they bought. You they praised as the father of good learning, as a Maecenas....

This book was dedicated a long time ago to one of your kinsmen by Erasmus. Now I beg you that you be my protector with him, that he may not bear me ill-will for having published it without his consent, but rather that he might accept my intention that it was printed by me in order to render a service to him and to you and to all students of good learning.

There follows a brief epistle from Siberch 'To the Reader' from which I quote:

Forgive me, dear reader, considering that I am an inexperienced beginner.... I freely confess that in printing this book I have made many mistakes. But I hope you will not hold this to be due to my carelessness, but to the extraordinarily bad state of the copy I was given and to the great difficulty of transcribing and correcting it, especially since I could not consult Erasmus himself, nor call in the help of a scholar....

Now, all this is very odd and irregular. What strikes us most is the lack of candour in everybody concerned. The deliberate reticence about the identity of the 'amicus' who furnished the copy and urged Siberch to publish it. I think Henry Bullock is very likely to have been responsible; he may have taken a copy when Erasmus was working on the book at Cambridge in 1511. The not-so-subtle idea of getting the Chancellor, Bishop Fisher, to accept the dedication of the book and thereby to place the whole illegitimate proceeding under the shield of a great man to whom

Erasmus had every reason to be grateful. The withholding of all scholarly help to the printer, and the consequent devolution of all responsibility on to the head of the craftsman. That this was in fact observed, and that Siberch was left entirely to his own resources of scholarship, can be clearly gathered from the Latin style of his letter, disfigured by some deplorable lapses of syntax which any don could have quite easily eliminated. Even Erasmus' furious indignation with the printer is not quite genuine. His letter to Beraldus was prefixed to Froben's edition of August 1522 and Froben, not Erasmus, was really the injured party. The publication of a 'new' work by Erasmus (however old) by any other firm than Froben's meant the breach of a contract between Erasmus and Froben. The Cambridge promoters must have known this and carefully refrained from asking Erasmus for a consent which he was not free to give. In reparation of this unintended breach of contract Froben could force Erasmus to undertake the uncongenial task of supplying a new, quite different 'genuine' *Ars Epistolandi*, and ultimately Froben probably did quite well out of the whole muddy affair. But that Erasmus did not really take the matter to heart can be gathered from his letter of 25 December 1525 to Robert Aldrich,* then at Cambridge, in which he includes Siberch among his 'veteres sodales' at Cambridge to whom he sends Christmas greetings.

For us the chief interest of the entire business may lie in the light it throws on the current conceptions of an author's and a publisher's rights in the early sixteenth century, and on the whole question of literary property. It was the age when the possibility that a literary composition might represent an asset of some commercial value first began to be recognised. Before the invention of printing the huge expense of preparing an additional copy precluded all thoughts of making a commercial profit out of multiplying a book in great demand. The Romans did so by means of slave labour. Each new copy had to be separately commissioned and paid for according to the materials employed and the quality of the calligrapher's work. After Gutenberg's invention became an established craft, that is to say by about 1470, the craftsmen of the printing trade still tended to look to some rich patron to finance the capital outlay of an edition of a few hundred or even a thousand copies, part of which he could use as presents, the rest to be sold as best it may, to recoup the initial cost and to provide an extra profit for the printer if all went well.

There were no established methods of marketing hundreds of copies of one and the same book. The idea of regarding a quantity of copies of one book as merchandise originated not with the printers but with the merchants. In the big commercial centres like Venice, Augsburg or Basle we first find the printers thriving because the local merchants and their agents gladly provided the organisation for distributing their products rapidly and on a world-wide scale. In the fifteenth century the attention of the book trade was still mainly concentrated on the standard books of established authority, for which a wide and hitherto unsatisfied demand could profitably be filled at the new low-cost prices. Occasional publications, generally of small size, of recent compositions by living authors were more often than not sponsored by the author himself or by some other interested party: job-printing, not publishing ventures. But it was soon discovered that there were authors whose writings met with so great a public response that a lot of money was being made by marketing their productions. Reprint after reprint was called for, but without such a thing as copyright there was no guarantee that the success of a new book would benefit its first publisher. Privileges obtained from the sovereign authority proved to be almost futile, especially in Germany and Italy, where the manifold political subdivisions of the country made a privilege obtained from the doge of Venice, let us say, quite ineffective in Bologna or in Milan. A book published with privilege at Basle could be reprinted at Strassburg or Augsburg with complete and fully legal immunity. German printers rarely troubled to go to the expense of obtaining a privilege which would protect them against local competition only, but left the wider market of the Empire and beyond entirely open.*

Erasmus of Rotterdam himself provides the earliest instance of a living author of such fame and wide appeal that every new publication of his, as soon as announced, could safely be regarded as a 'best seller'. Consequently he was pursued by all the publisher-printers who could reach him, seeking to obtain his next composition. For a new work by Erasmus was a certain success—within a narrow time limit; that is to say until another printer could get hold of a copy and issue a reprint. We find Thierry Martens at Louvain, Froben at Basle and Schürer at Strassburg reprinting each other's first editions within one month. Under such circumstances the monetary inducement they could offer to the author for the priority was not very substantial. Still it was worth a lot of trouble, and we hear

of Thierry Martens walking a hundred miles all through the night from
Louvain to Antwerp and back again in a vain chase of Erasmus and of
some fresh copy from him. Finally that ingenious man, Froben of Basle,
solved the problem by gently kidnapping the author himself. By 1521 he
had the frail, ageing bachelor installed in an apartment in his own house
and he provided him with an excellent cook-housekeeper. From then on
he had no more trouble in securing all Erasmus' writings as they flowed
from his pen.

We possess a valuable study on Erasmus' relations with his printers by
P. S. Allen,* in which he has collected all the references from his correspondence that bear on the matter. From that paper, better than from any
multiplicity of other sources, we can gather some conception of the mental
attitudes of the sixteenth century facing the novel ethical—not yet legal—
problems of literary property rights. The author's right to dispose freely
of his productions was never questioned and every slight alteration or
addition he chose to make to his published text left him free again to hand
a new edition to another publisher. The venturer on the first edition,
perhaps with many copies still remaining unsold, could resent such a
proceeding but he saw no means of inhibiting it. As for the competition
between the producers of reprints, this was a free for all fight with no
tricks barred, and there was no possibility of securing an advantage except
by being quick off the mark and possessing a good organisation for
advance sales before publication. Under such conditions the author's
remuneration necessarily remained very low and somewhat precarious,
and it was not till the establishment of effective copyright legislation that
a popular author could make sure of a living without having recourse to
the generosity of patrons.

On another Erasmus item printed by Siberch, of which only one leaf
has survived, I need not dwell at length. It is an edition of the *De Octo
Orationis Partium Constructione*,* the Latin school-grammar commissioned
by John Colet for his newly founded school, St Paul's. The first High
Master, William Lily, drew it up and submitted it to Erasmus for revision
with the result that the book as published cannot be regarded either as the
work of Lily or of Erasmus.* The first edition is anonymous and printed
by Pynson at London in 1513.* Innumerable reprints followed both here
and on the Continent, mostly with Erasmus' name, since he had published
a revised version with Froben at Basle in 1515 with a preface in which he

candidly discloses Lily's share in the book.* It became the most generally used school-grammar in the progressive schools of Northern Europe, and it is not surprising that Siberch reprinted it for use in the Cambridge schools.

The most important by far of Siberch's books, and perhaps the only one to be proud of, is Thomas Linacre's translation of Galen on the Temperaments. It is also the most substantial, a quarto of eighty-two leaves. Linacre was not a Cambridge but an Oxford man; there is no indication in the book of the reasons that induced him to entrust it to the new Cambridge press. It is the first edition of Linacre's version as the title claims, and it is dedicated to Pope Leo X with whom, as Linacre recalls, he sat as a fellow-pupil under Poliziano in Florence learning Greek (1486).

Linacre is most generally remembered as the founder and first president of the Royal College of Physicians (1518), and therewith as the creator of the examining and licensing authority which from the start regulated and still regulates the admission to the medical profession. In his lifetime however Linacre was a European celebrity, not as a practising physician, but as one of the earliest and foremost scholars to use his knowledge of Greek for translating the Greek medical and scientific books into Latin: Galen, Proclus and Aristotle himself.* Linacre's published Latin versions of Galen form an impressive series. The *De Sanitate Tuenda* and the big *Methodus Medendi*, both dedicated to King Henry VIII, came out in Paris in 1517 and 1519. The Cambridge *De Temperamentis* of 1521 is the third. There follow three others printed by Pynson in London in 1523-4, the year of Linacre's death. All these versions were frequently reprinted on the Continent.

I think it requires some explanation why at that period an eminent physician should become world-famous not for any contribution to medical knowledge (of which we hear nothing) but for making a Greek medical author accessible in Latin. Throughout the Middle Ages all medical teaching, as far as it was not purely traditional and empirical, was based on the Arabic text-books of Avicenna, Rhazes, Mesue, etc., which became known in Latin partly through Spanish translators, partly through the school of Salerno. These Arabic books were still the current source of medical doctrine in Linacre's day, and we possess plenty of incunable editions of their Latin versions. Whatever their merits or shortcomings,

these Arabs do by no means conceal the fact that they derive their knowledge from the ancient Greeks. On every page they quote as their
authorities Hippocrates and Galen and there must have been many
medieval doctors who knew that a certain precept was vouched for by
'Tegni Galeni' without being aware of the fact that 'tegni' is nothing but
the Greek word 'techne' and that 'Galeni' was a physician from Asia
Minor who wrote in Greek at Rome and died A.D. 201.

When the humanist 'Revival of Learning' had produced a fair number
of scholars with a command of Greek, the medical world eagerly demanded
that the Greek originals of the ancient teachers be found and properly
translated. They were convinced that the infidel Saracens had misunder-
stood and garbled the true teaching of Hippocrates and Galen, and that
a recourse to the genuine texts would bring forth an epoch-making
enlightenment on the fundamentals of medical knowledge. Hence the
zeal with which the translators got to work when Greek codices of the
medical classics became available, and hence the gratitude and esteem of
the scholarly world for those who, like Linacre, made the real teaching of
the Greeks accessible in a language they could understand.

Seen in the perspective of later developments, the 'revelations' of the
Greek sources proved a disappointment. The Arabs had not materially mis-
represented their Greek masters. Galenic medicine, whether based on
Arabic text-books or on the Greek originals, continued to dominate
medical practice with its doctrines of the four temperaments, of the
different humours of the body, of hot and of frigid substances. Still,
the confrontation of the old Arabs with the newly won true versions,
the fierce battles between the traditionalist Arabists and the 'modern'
humanist physicians, roused the critical spirit of the age to new departures,
to original research and experiment. Without Linacre and his fellow translators, the stimulus for Vesalius, Paré and the other sixteenth-century
pioneers of modern medicine would have been lacking.

It is characteristic of the 'humanists' and the linguistic preoccupations of
the generation of Erasmus, that Linacre should have spent the last twenty
years of his life (apart from his practice) not in medical research or in
further translations, but in the elaboration of a truly up-to-date Latin
syntax, and that the De Emendata Structura Latini Sermonis, printed by
Pynson in 1524 shortly after his death, should have become his most
famous and his most universally accepted work. All Continental humanist

schools based their teaching on it and reprints follow each other in Paris and in Germany till near the end of the century.*

In a different context* I had occasion to point to the fact, often over-looked, that the humanist generations of the first century of printing by no means confined their search for ancient texts worth editing to the Greek and Roman classics, but that in investigating the ancient MSS. in the old libraries they often chanced to meet with medieval books that appealed to them, and which they proudly exhibited as relics of the past worth reading by their contemporaries. Even in Siberch's limited output of ten titles there is a striking example of such a first edition of a book centuries old. The little quarto of twenty leaves in which Siberch for the first time calls himself 'primus utriusque linguae in Anglia impressor' contains the *Sermo de Sacramento Altaris* by Baldwin, archbishop of Canterbury, who accompanied Richard Cœur de Lion to the Holy Land and was killed at the siege of Acre in 1190. Whether Gerald de Barri (Giraldus Cambrensis) was justified in saying of him that he was 'better as a monk than as an abbot, better as a bishop than as an archbishop' I have no means of judging. The Cambridge edition of this twelfth-century sermon is dedicated to the same Nicholas West, bishop of Ely, who had accepted the dedication of Bullock's *Lucian*. This identity of the recipient illustrates the attitude, I would suggest, which made a newly translated Greek piece and a newly exhumed medieval sermon equally acceptable reading matter for the curious of the early sixteenth century. Far too many writers on Renaissance subjects go wrong in drawing a rigid dividing line between the humanists interested in the pagan classics and the reactionaries persisting in medieval barbarism. A great part of the labours of the early translators from the Greek was devoted to the Byzantine theologians (writing before the schism of course), and many of the most eminent humanist scholars like Ambrogio Traversari and others shunned the pagan poets and directed their research exclusively to the Pythagorean and Neo-Platonist philo-sophers, in which they found much to enrich their religious meditations.

Bradshaw, in his chronological enumeration of Siberch's impressions, placed second, immediately after Bullock's *Oratio*, a quarto of twelve leaves to which he refers as St Augustine, *Sermo*. This appellation, con-venient from the cataloguing librarian's point of view, is justifiable because

St Augustine is really the only author's name discoverable in the book. It is however misleading, for St Augustine only appears as the author of a sermon on the brevity of human life placed as an appendix in the end, occupying the last seven pages only. The bulk of the book, the preceding seventeen pages, consists of an anonymous *Epistola of a True Christian*, exhorting all and sundry to repentance, for the end of the world is rapidly approaching. This piece may be by a Cambridge author, it may equally well be a reprint of a Continental tract; it has at its conclusion the date 1521, which is also the date of imprint; that is to say it was a recent composition. It bases its prediction of impending doom on astrological arguments, on the famous conjunction of all the seven planets in the sign of Pisces in the year 1524, which was widely viewed with terror as presaging a new Deluge. This so-called Augustine therefore belongs to the enormous mass of pamphlets devoted to upholding or controverting the current prophecy of a universal Deluge in 1524.*

Within a year or two Siberch printed another item, the *Prognostication*, described by F. S. Ferguson in the *Transactions of the Cambridge Bibliographical Society*, I, pp. 41–5, which refers to the same gloomy prediction.

A curious detail of that 'St Augustine' does not seem to have been noted so far. On the last page it carries a poem in five distichs: 'Joannis Duncelli, Hammelburgensis, in saeculi hujus amatorem Decastychon.' This 'Duncellus' is not completely unknown. He must have been a kinsman of the Basle printer John Froben (who was also Hammelburgensis), and he seems to have accompanied Erasmus as his boy servant to England in 1515. He is mentioned in a letter from Beatus Rhenanus to Erasmus dated 17 April 1515: 'Froben says he never had any instructions from Duncellus to send him clothes...' and further on, 'If however you have incurred any expenses in buying clothes or anything else for Duncellus, Froben reliably promised to refund them to you.'*

It is quite possible, but by no means certain, that Duncellus whose vernacular name would probably be Hans Dünkel, stayed on in Cambridge after Erasmus' departure and may have worked in Siberch's printing office.

Martin Luther was excommunicated on 10 December 1520 and all his books were condemned to be burned. This decree was exactly and punctiliously carried out in many cities of Germany and the Netherlands.

In London Luther's books were solemnly burned in front of St Paul's on 12 May 1521, Henry Bullock being one of the commissioners in charge of the ceremony.

On the very same day there was a debate on the matter in the House of Lords in which John Fisher, Chancellor of Cambridge University, as bishop of Rochester, made a speech. This address was promptly turned into Latin by Richard Pace, the King's Secretary. Pace's Latin version was handed to Siberch by Nicholas Wilson* and appeared in print with the date 1521 on the title, but according to the present system of beginning the year, early in 1522.

It is almost as if among the ten meagre titles of Siberch's œuvre there *had* to be at least one to echo the great cause of the moment, Luther's defiance, which had just begun to keep all the printing presses humming on the Continent. The Lutheran Reformation was the first of all movements to enlist the services of the printers to an unprecedented extent and every kind of printed matter, from the learned theological treatise to the most scurrilous propaganda sheet began to pour from the presses.

However, Siberch's quarto was not in intention a contribution to the controversy that was shaking the world; rather it conforms to the general pattern of academic occasional pieces to which his other books belong. It is an elegant offering of a smooth Ciceronian version of Fisher's speech, a tribute from the King's Secretary to the eminent prelate, a display of distinguished Latin style bestowed by Richard Pace on his friend's parliamentary eloquence.

The last of Siberch's dated impressions, the *Hermathena* of 8 December 1522, is perhaps the most significant, though in some respects the most mysterious of his products. It is in form and in subject the most explicit manifesto of the humanist movement issued in England. An allegory closely modelled on Lucian's *Dialogues of the Gods*, it tells how the goddesses of Wisdom and of Eloquence were expelled from Rome by the armies of 'Desidia', Laziness, and her followers: the women, the nobility, the pseudo-philosophers* and the quibbling lawyers.* Eloquence flees to the gods of Olympus and to the Elysian fields; there we hear speeches by Julius Caesar, by Cicero and by Servius Sulpicius in support of her cause. An army is raised, Desidia is defeated, Sophia freed, and together with Eloquence sails to England where they are cherished by the great King Henry VIII.

This strange exercise in Lucianic mythological phantasy, without any trace of Lucianic wit, is dedicated to Richard Pace,* the King's Secretary and at that time next to Cardinal Wolsey the most powerful man at Court. His is the Latin translation of the Chancellor, John Fisher's speech in the House of Lords which Siberch had printed earlier in the same year, 1522; on its title-page Pace is termed 'vir Grece et Latine peritissimus'. Pace was indeed a keen Greek scholar who, as early as 1504, then a very young man, had made a public speech at Venice in praise of Greek studies. Soon after 1510 he dedicated to Cardinal Bainbridge, in whose service he was till his death in 1514, a translation of two of Plutarch's *Moralia* together with Lucian's *Vita Demonactis*, which was printed by Jac. Mazochius at Rome; neither the dedication nor the book bears a precise date. In 1517 he published with Froben at Basle his *De Fructu qui ex Doctrina Percipitur*, dedicated to John Colet, whom he succeeded as Dean of St Paul's. This book, which gave great offence to Erasmus (see *Op. Ep.* III, p. 218) is of interest to us as an English scholar's exposition of the value of humanist and especially Greek studies. It dwells particularly on the prejudice of the English nobility, all too keen on hunting and on horses, against learning and 'good letters', a theme recalled in the *Hermathena*.*

Who is the author of the *Hermathena*? He calls himself Papyrius Geminus Eleates, a beautiful humanist appellation, which may hide any vernacular name you can think of. There were no rules that the humanists observed in choosing a fine sounding literary pseudonym in substitution of their family name and it is useless to try translating back. 'It would be interesting to know more about Papyrius Geminus', Bradshaw wrote in 1886.* I am afraid I cannot carry the matter any further; the identity of this Papyrius still remains unrevealed. But there are a few observations I would like to make which perhaps some day may lead a skilful antiquary to find the solution to this puzzle.

As Bradshaw noted there exists another book in which the name occurs: Edward Powell's *Propugnaculum*, printed by Pynson in 1523 (*S.T.C.* 20140), an anti-Lutheran tract. This has a Preface to the Reader by Papyrius Geminus Eliates in which he praises Henry VIII as Defensor Fidei. The author Edward Powell was a resident canon of Salisbury.

About the turn of the year 1521–2 Richard Pace, who accumulated many benefices, was made prebendary of Coombe in the chapter of Salisbury, and left England immediately afterwards for Rome on the mission of getting Wolsey elected Pope. The *Hermathena* has two dedicatory epistles from Geminus to Pace, that at the beginning dated from London, February 1522, that at the end dated 'Comi pridie Nonas Septembris 1522'. Bradshaw thought that 'Comi' meant Como in Italy; I believe it is intended for Coombe Bissett in Wiltshire. It is a possible hypothesis that Papyrius Geminus was appointed by Pace to the living of Coombe when he obtained the prebend, and that the dedication of the *Hermathena* may be a gesture of gratitude for the benefice. But I have so far not been able to obtain information on the identity of the vicar in 1522. The fact that in the following year, 1523, Geminus' name appears in a book by a canon of Salisbury seems to point to the probability that he remained in residence there.

On the other hand Geminus calls himself Eleates in the *Hermathena*, Eliates in Powell's *Propugnaculum*, and this makes it plausible, *prima facie*, that he personally originated from the diocese of Ely.

Lastly I very hesitatingly come forward with another suggestion. A man who called himself Geminus in Latin may possibly have been called something like Twin or perhaps (?) Twyne in English. In his second letter to Pace in the *Hermathena* there is a passage in which he declares that little book to be a preliminary exercise for a History of England he was composing: 'auspicaturus historiam pro nostris Anglibritannis.'

Now there exists a history, *De Rebus Albionicis, Britannicis atque Anglicis, Joannis Twini Bolingdunensis*, which was published after the author's death (in 1581) by his son Thomas Twyne of Corpus Christi College, Oxford. It is printed in London by Bollifant in 1590 (*S.T.C.* 24407). This John Twyne, who is listed in *D.N.B.*, was a schoolmaster at Canterbury, and I can find no connection between him and the diocese of Salisbury or of Ely. Chronologically it is possible that a man who died in 1581 was planning his History of England as early as 1522. But I think all these vague guesses are not much use, and we can only hope that some lucky find some day may bring to light the identity of Papyrius Geminus.

Siberch stopped printing in 1522 or 1523; no attempt was made to set a press to work in Cambridge till 1584. Similarly in Oxford there was no printing in the sixteenth century before 1585.* The reasons for this inactivity are fairly plain.

An undertaking like Siberch's was not conceived on a commercial basis; it was established on a scheme of patronage. If any thought was given to the permanence of the enterprise, it must have been expected that a sufficient number of well-to-do scholars would constantly be prepared to come forward with commissions for the sake of seeing themselves or their friends in print. The economics of publishing, still somewhat mysterious today, must have been very obscure and unexplored in the period of the infancy of printing. The demand for printed matter was not thought of as that of a wide public anxious to buy certain kinds of books. The people who paid for the printers' costs were the men who wanted to distribute free copies of their own compositions to their friends and patrons, just as we now demand two dozen offprints of any contribution we make to a periodical, and sometimes are even willing to pay for them.

Such constant willingness to sacrifice money for the sake of fame or notoriety could never be expected to last indefinitely. Most early academic presses were very shortlived. When the printers found that the orders were drying up, that their over-enthusiastic backers did not make good their promises of a regular flow of printing orders, they looked to commercial publishing as a more likely means of making a livelihood. But that sort of enterprise could not be carried on in a university town. It required first and foremost a good system of transportation and communication with as wide a sector of the book-buying world as possible. Publishing was always a mass producing industry, and a rapid and extensive distribution was always an essential necessity. Therefore only those printers could flourish who had settled in the big commercial cities from which an edition of a thousand or more copies could easily be shipped off in all directions.

The Italian university towns provide an instructive parallel to the lethargy of Cambridge and Oxford printing in the first half of the sixteenth century. Next to Bologna, Padua was the most frequented university in Italy. In the fifteenth century Paduan printing starts in the grand manner with a wealthy patrician, Bartolomeo di Valdezoccho, employing a Prussian craftsman to print Petrarch and Boccaccio for him. He is followed by an even more impressive undertaking fully worthy of the greatest scientific university of the period: the grand edition of the Latin Aristotle with Averroes' commentary. Five big folio volumes of it come out between 1472 and 1474. They were the work of a reputed painter and artist in wood-mosaic (tarsia) Laurentius Canozius; the considerable funds required for such an ambitious production were provided by a nobleman from Vicenza, Joannes Philippus Aurelianus and his brothers, no doubt members of the university. After that Padua printing gradually ebbs off. In the eighties of the fifteenth century the academic aspect of Padua printing is mainly represented by the thin little quartos of Matheus Cerdonis de Windischgraetz. The British Museum possesses only two books printed at Padua in the 1490's and apparently only one printed between 1500 and 1520 (see Isaac 13836) and that from a monastery press. Padua was in Venetian territory and the great commercial printing centre Venice was much too close to permit a favourable development of printing in competition with it. All the sixteenth-century Paduan scientific and medical text-books are printed in Venice.

As Padua was too near Venice, so the University of Pavia was too close to Milan. After an imposing series chiefly of legal and medical text-books printed before 1490, the output of the Pavia presses diminishes in importance and size. The two firms that carry on into the period 1500–20 print a few medical books of lesser volume, but it is obvious that the former confidence had gone out of that business. Similarly at Siena the grand legal folios of Henricus de Harlem cease in 1495; in the early sixteenth century there is only one press at Siena turning out little pamphlets, chiefly in Italian.

Bologna appears to be the only Italian university town where printing, and specifically humanist printing, flourished in the first quarter of the sixteenth century. Philippus Beroaldus and Jo. B. Pius were teachers of wide celebrity and also prolific authors and editors. They kept the presses of the various members of the de Benedictis family and that of Bened. Hectoris supplied with titles that commanded a ready sale, not only in Bologna itself, but also among their numerous foreign pupils then scattered all over the world. Although we know that Bologna at that time was the home of several teachers of Greek to whom pupils came from far and wide, and although Greek type was used for quotations, etc. in many of these books, we do not find a single wholly Greek text-book printed there. No doubt the Aldine editions were used for these courses.

When Siberch had convinced himself that there was no future for his press at Cambridge, he seems to have left the country, probably going to Antwerp. We do not know what became of him after 1523, but some of his ornaments turn up in the hands of Antwerp printers.*

II

THE EMPHASIS ON GREEK

THE four lines of Greek proverbs at the end of Bullock's *Lucian* and Siberch's proud claim to be 'primus utriusque Linguae in Anglia impressor' demand some comment. What was the situation in Cambridge in 1521 that made the installation of a press equipped with Greek type a matter of urgency and a cause of pride?

Certainly not a demand for Greek books. Not only did Siberch himself never print one, but no other English printer ventured on such an enterprise for another seventy years.* What little demand there was for such abstruse reading matter was easily satisfied by importation from the few Continental presses active in this field.

It is necessary to present as briefly as feasible a wide survey of the development of Greek studies in Western Europe so as to understand what may have been the dominant motive in the minds of Croke, Bullock and their friends when they insisted on a Greek press at the precise moment, 1520, when it took shape—as a potentiality at least. We are constrained to go far afield, both in time and space, for it is a European movement, not a local Cambridge phenomenon, that we meet in this manifestation. A movement of European scope, and 'movements', as you may have observed, gain their impetus more often and more strongly from their direction against some established practice or institution, rather than from a devotion to their professed aims.

The insistence on the necessity of some knowledge of the Greek classics in their original language forms part of the movement generally called 'humanism'; the postulate that 'a man who has no Greek' cannot be regarded as an educated gentleman persists from Guarino da Verona to Gladstone's day. 'Humanism' has become an awkward word, sadly debased by the admixture of extraneous philosophic implications, which have caused many German and American professors to write articles in order to explain to each other what humanism really means. We will leave it at that, and baldly state that Greek teaching, which Petrarch still found so desirable but unobtainable, began in Medicean Florence, in 1396 to be precise. Throughout the fifteenth century it is in Italy and in Italy only that Greek is regularly taught by various scholars, both Italian and Greek immigrants, and a considerable body of people able to read and to translate from the Greek continues to exist. Fifteenth-century Greek teaching remains on the whole entirely disconnected with the universities, even in the quite numerous cases when a teacher of Greek chooses to establish his residence in a university town and to seek his pupils among the student body, as Aurispa did at Bologna in 1425.

The Italians who taught Greek in Latin, not in the vernacular, and whose instruction could therefore be followed by pupils from any country, were mostly maintained by the generosity of some prince, or else they depended for their livelihood entirely on the fees they collected from their pupils. Poliziano at Florence, Filelfo at Milan, Guarino at Ferrara received their remuneration from the court, and their teaching was a 'courtly' education intended to form the minds of young men aspiring to diplomatic or administrative employment. Polish, elegance, fluency of expression, familiarity with the great authors of the Classical past, these were the aims of the training they gave, not the professional teaching required to enter a corporation of practising lawyers or physicians, which was the province of the universities. To supplement their income these Italian Graecists were busily occupied in translating the newly discovered Greek authors into Latin, and dedicating their versions to generous patrons for which they received very substantial 'presents'.

These Renaissance translations from the Greek into Latin have perhaps been unduly neglected. They may have appeared to a later age as pedantic exercises of scholarly proficiency, turning a text from one unintelligible language into another unintelligible language. Such a view is completely erroneous, I feel sure, and the importance of these Latin versions in the development of European thought is quite considerable. Not only was the number of manuscripts of a Greek author available in the West extremely small, but they were jealously treasured by their owners, and by no means easily accessible. Competent copyists of Greek texts were rare and highly rewarded.

Moreover the circle of scholars who possessed more than the rudiments of Greek, who could read the Greek originals with ease and enjoyment, always remained very restricted. But in the fifteenth and sixteenth centuries the literate public who read nothing but Latin, and would hardly have cared to read a book in any vernacular language, was vast, international and practically coextensive with the entire educated population of Europe. Their curiosity about the newly recovered Greek authors led to an immediate demand for Latin versions and, with the introduction of printing, to repeated editions of the works that appealed to them. These printed Latin editions precede by a long time the appearance of the Greek originals, and it is in their Latin form rather than in the Greek that the thought of ancient Hellas made its impact on European letters.*

The multiplicity of existing translations and the frequency of early printed editions can show us in what directions the interests of the reading public between 1400 and 1520 were mainly engaged. The sublime poetic qualities of the tragedians and lyric poets remained obscure to them; Aeschylus, Sophocles, Euripides, as well as Pindar, Sappho, Anacreon, etc., were not turned into Latin, or if any early translations of them exist they are still hidden in manuscripts. The exception that proves the rule is provided by that very exceptional man Erasmus, who translated Euripides' *Iphigenia in Aulis* and *Hecuba* into Latin verse, and dedicated them to Archbishop Warham in 1506.* The more general attitude of incomprehension and indifference of the earlier generations of humanists is perhaps best exemplified by Angelo Poliziano (1454–94), 'the first teacher in Italy whose mastery of Greek was equal to that of the Greek immigrants', the man who taught Grocyn and Linacre what Greek they knew.* In 1486 Poliziano gave a course of lectures at Florence on the history of poetry from Homer to Boccaccio, and he introduced it by one of his *Sylvae*, a versified abstract of his theme. In this *Sylva* the three masters of Greek tragedy are dismissed with one verse apiece, purporting to tell how each of them met his death: Aeschylus by a tortoise falling on his head, Sophocles by a shock of joy at the success of a play, Euripides mauled by wild dogs in Macedonia.

Clearly it was not for their literary qualities that the fifteenth-century public sought to know the Greek authors, but for the factual contributions they could make to scientific knowledge and, above all, for the philosophical wisdom to be found in their writings. Aristotle, of course, was known in Latin translations, partly from very early times, but mainly from the thirteenth century and the days of Thomas Aquinas. The teaching of the University of Paris was based on Aristotle from its very inception. But he finds new translators in the Renaissance period who present the world with a new and very different text. The fifteenth-century Aristotle of Argyropulos, of George of Trebizond, or of Leonardo Bruni of Arezzo gave an entirely new comprehension of peripatetic thought.

Plato, on the other hand, was a novelty when the first Greek codices reached Italy about 1400. As a newcomer and a more ancient sage than Aristotle himself, he gained a fervent welcome from the humanists, and the second half of the fifteenth century saw a violent partisanship and controversy between the pro-Platonic humanists and the pro-Aristotelian scientists. The Italian scholars soon began to make translations of single books, the industrious Leonardo Bruni of Arezzo being among the first to bring out a Latin *Apologia Socratis* and a *Gorgias*, as well as a *Criton*, all before 1420. Pier Candido Decembrio dedicated his version of the *Republic* to Duke Humphrey of Gloucester in 1440. By 1477 the Florentine Platonist Marsilio Ficino has completed his translation of the whole corpus of Plato's writings, and by April 1485 the first Latin edition of Plato's *Works* was printed and published at Florence in two volumes. Ficino's Latin Plato was the standard text which the Renaissance period knew; it was reprinted at Venice in 1491, and again in 1517, and further editions succeeded each other throughout the sixteenth century. The Greek original text was not printed till 1513; one of that tremendous series of editiones principes of Greek authors by which Aldus Manutius of Venice has immortalised his name. No second Greek edition came out in Italy at all, at least not for centuries. The second Greek Plato was that printed by Valderus at Basle in 1534. When we speak of Plato's influence on Renaissance thought, which was considerable, it is to Ficino's Latin Plato we must look for the source of its knowledge.

The most powerful and generous patronage for the translators from the Greek emanated from successive humanist occupants of the papal throne, especially Pope Nicholas V (1447–55)—Tommaso Parentucelli of Sarzana —who was passionately interested in recuperating the Greek authors from the East, and in seeing them placed side by side with their Latin versions in his library. He had been librarian to Cosimo de' Medici, and can be regarded as the founder of both the Medicean and the Vatican Libraries.*

His interests, besides Aristotle and the Greek Fathers (Chrysostom, Eusebius, Basilius, etc.) were mainly concentrated on the historians. For him Lorenzo Valla translated Thucydides (printed at Treviso, *c.* 1483) and Herodotus (printed at Venice, 1474 and Rome, 1475). Poggio turned the first five books of Diodorus Siculus into Latin (printed at Bologna, 1472);

Perotti made a translation of Polybius (printed at Rome, 1472), Pier Candido Decembrio of Appian (Venice, 1472). For Nicholas V also Guarino translated the *Geography* of Strabo, which happens to be the earliest of all these translations to appear in print (Rome, 1469). The *Geography* of Ptolemy had already been translated by Giacomo Angeli da Scarparia for Pope Alexander V in 1410, and was printed at Vicenza in 1475. None of these authors came out in the original Greek text before 1500.

The *History of Greek Philosophy* by Diogenes Laertius was translated by Ambrogio Traversari before 1439, and appeared in print from a Roman press by 1472; the original Greek text did not come out before 1533. Laertius took the place of the fourteenth-century Walter Burley, whose *Dictes and Sayings* had until then supplied what information Europe possessed on the ancient philosophers.

It was not metaphysical speculation that the Renaissance reader looked for in the Greek authors, nor discussions of formal logic, which had become abhorrent to him through the official teaching of dialectics in the universities. What he wanted to find was the teaching of practical ethics, of statecraft and of sound government, which had raised the ancient city-states to that eminence of dignity upon which he looked with admiration. Repelled by the medieval barbarism of the age of the Condottieri, he hoped to learn from the Greeks the guiding principles of a civilised society based on the rule of law. Too long had the world suffered from brutal oppression by feudal lords and their lawless camp-followers, contending for power against each other and exercising the 'administration' of their territories mainly by confiscations, executions and banishments. The problem in the forefront of public concern was that of good government, of the establishment of public authorities deserving of respect, of the duties and limitations of the sovereign power. From Egidio Colonna's *De Regimine Principum* (written about 1300) down to Erasmus' *Institutio Principis Christiani* (1516), the central theme of speculation and discussion remained the ethical and legal definition of the rights and duties of the sovereign.

The dominant interest in statecraft and civic duty is clearly reflected in the choice of Greek texts attracting the earliest translators and soon disseminated in numerous Latin editions. We hear little nowadays of Isocrates, an Attic orator of the fourth century, and yet his speeches are among the few Greek classics printed in Greek before Aldus began his great series of Greek first editions; they came out in Milan in 1493. Especially his *Oratio ad Nicoclem de Regno* and that *ad Demonicum de Modo bene Vivendi* were again and again translated by a succession of scholars, and the total of their early Latin editions must amount to a formidable figure. Versions by Bernardo Giustiniani (1408–89) and by Rudolph Agricola (1444–85) exist in fifteenth-century editions. Othmar Luscinius made a fresh translation at Strassburg (1515), Erasmus himself at Louvain (1516, 1518), the Spaniard Vives in 1523. Sir Thomas Elyot's *Doctrinal of Princes*, printed by Berthelet in 1534, is but an English version of the *Nicocles*. Even earlier than Isocrates, Dion Chrysostom's treatise *De Regno* in a Latin version by Francesco Piccolomini issues from Valdarfer's press at Venice about 1471.

The duties of the good prince can also be defined by presenting the bad prince, the tyrant, as an example to be detested. Xenophon's *Hiero vel de Vita Tyrannica* was translated before 1417 by Leonardi Bruni and, after several other versions, by Erasmus in 1530. But the favourite tyrant of the Renaissance was undoubtedly Phalaris, whose curt and 'tyrannical' letters were accepted as genuine enunciations of the cruel ruler of Agrigentum. They were translated into Latin by Francesco Griffolini of Arezzo* about 1450 from a big Greek volume in the library of Pope Nicholas V (now Vat. gr. 1309) which Ciriaco d'Ancona had brought from Mount Athos.

His Latin version was first printed at Rome by Ulrich Han without date, but before rather than after 1470. The number of reprints of this Latin *Phalaris* is very large; Hain, Copinger and Reichling between them describe thirty-seven different editions before 1500. Wherever printing began under the patronage of the humanists, we generally meet a *Phalaris* among the earliest products of the press. The Paris Sorbonne press issued a *Phalaris* in 1472. In Bologna, Brescia, Treviso and Florence Phalaris was printed before 1480. Even at Oxford Theodoric Rood and Thomas Hunt published Griffolini's *Phalaris* in 1485.*

For notable examples of statesmanship the Renaissance reader turned to Plutarch's *Lives*. In the original Greek they were not printed till 1517, but when, before 1470, J. A. Campanus, bishop of Teramo, conceived the plan of editing them in Latin, he found most of them available in translations dating from a much earlier generation. His edition was published at Rome in, or soon after, 1470. Guarino da Verona, Franciscus Philelphus, Lapo de

Castiglionchio the younger, and Leonardo Bruni of Arezzo between them supplied the bulk of the versions included. The first Roman Plutarch was soon reprinted at Strassburg by the so-called R-printer, Adolph Rusch, and by Jenson at Venice in 1478. Further Venetian editions and Paris editions from Badius' press adhered with minor improvements to the Roman collection without thorough recourse to the Greek original.

Plutarch's other writings were brought to the West by G. Aurispa in 1423 in one big volume, which became known under the title of *Moralia*, and was first printed in Greek by Aldus in 1509. Of the ninety-two different pieces it comprises, a number had been translated and published in Latin long before that date. Franciscus Philelphus' version of the *Apophthegmata*, dedicated to Pope Nicholas V, was printed in 1471 at Venice and within two years reappeared at Utrecht from the press of Ketelaer and de Leempt under the title *Dicterie Plutarchi*. The treatise on education in Guarino da Verona's version *De Liberis Educandis*, first printed at Parma in 1472, became one of the programmatic books of the humanist movement, and went through a multiplicity of editions. Guillaume Budé also must have had access to a Greek manuscript; as early as 1505 he published through Badius Ascensius his version of *De Tranquillitate Animi* and of *De Fortuna Romanorum*, and in 1506 that of *De Placitis Philosophorum*.

With the appearance of the Aldine edition of 1509 the storehouse of Plutarch's short essays was opened to all the world, and hardly any competent Greek scholar anywhere failed to choose one or the other of them for translation as a slight offering to some friend or patron. Erasmus was among the first to use them as New Year presents, 'ut mos est apud Anglos'.* He dedicated the *Warning against Flatterers* to King Henry VIII (1513) and *How to Keep in Good Health* to Sir John Yonge, Master of the Rolls (printed by Pynson in 1513). In 1518 he sent *The Way to Make Use of One's Enemies* to Cardinal Wolsey. A small collection of Erasmus' versions from Plutarch was published by Froben at Basle in 1514, by Thierry Martens at Louvain in 1515.

Richard Pace offered translations of two such essays by Plutarch, together with Lucian's *Life of Demonax*, to Cardinal Christopher Bainbridge, whose secretary he was until his death in 1514, when he himself succeeded him as Henry VIII's ambassador to the Pope; they were printed by Mazochius at Rome, and reprinted with further additions from Plutarch at Venice in 1522.

Willibald Pirckheimer of Nürnberg, Erasmus' and Dürer's friend, published three versions from Plutarch in 1513, 1515 and 1517. But these few examples by no means exhaust the tale of translators of Plutarch's *Moralia*.

Amid all this high seriousness it is a relief to find that among the rediscovered Greek authors it was Lucian of Samosata who made the widest appeal. He was among the very earliest to be translated,* among the earliest to be printed in Latin (*c.* 1470 at Rome), and the number of Lucian editions before 1536 in Greek, Latin, Italian, French, German and Czech comes to over two hundred, according to a bibliography I have attempted to compile.

The reasons for this rapid and world-wide popularity are not difficult to comprehend. It was a pleasant shock to find that a forbidding-looking stout vellum codex in Greek script could contain so much matter for laughter, so much fantasy and joyous persiflage. The irreverent scoffer at the pagan gods could never be held to offend against the established dogma; but the attitude of irreverence and irony itself was a surprise when met in an ancient manuscript, and it opened entirely new possibilities for literary compositions in a manner not yet heard of. As the eager readers and translators came to know Lucian's *Dialogues* one by one, there must have been many a chuckle of recognition when they noticed that second-century Syria and fifteenth-century Europe were not so different after all. Those grimy 'philosophers' in ragged clothes who lived as parasites at the rich man's table; how could you help being reminded of the Friars haunting the banquets of the noble and the wealthy? Their absurd meta-physical disputes paraded as superior learning, well...had you not been obliged to listen to similar 'table-talk' in the Latin quarter of Paris?

The impression Lucian made on Renaissance Europe was immense, long-lasting and of great consequence. All the living masterpieces of the early sixteenth century are echoes of Lucian: Erasmus' *Praise of Folly*, More's *Utopia*, Rabelais' *Pantagruel*, and a thousand feebler imitations stand as witnesses to the dominance of the Syrian satirist over the best brains of Europe.*

It is a strange thing to realise that the magnificent effort of the Aldine editions of the Greek authors marks the end, not the beginning, of humanism in Italy. They are the culmination of the endeavours and wishes of a whole century; but their sequel is negligible in Italy. They bear their fruit beyond the Alps.

With the death of Pope Leo X in 1521 the spirit of humanist enthusiasm departed from Italy. The devotees of Hellas and of Rome lost their ambition to 'imitate' the ancients by composing original works to rank with Homer and Cicero, and classical learning soon became dry-as-dust philology or archaeological antiquarianism. Leo's own secretary, Cardinal Pietro Bembo, the most eminent member of Aldus' Venetian Neacademia, whose letters of state had been models of Ciceronian style, wrote his *Della Volgar Lingua* (1525), and became the patron and creator of Italian prose as a means of elegant expression.

But before Leo died he not only remodelled the university of Rome, the Sapienza, in a humanist spirit, establishing several professorial chairs of classical learning (1513), he added, in 1515, an entirely new foundation, the college of Greeks on the Quirinal. For its head he recalled from France the same Janus Lascaris who had been at Florence in 1494 the first editor of the *Greek Anthology*. A Greek press was soon established to provide the required books; it was run by Zachary Kallierges, who had been Aldus' only serious rival as a Greek printer at Venice. This press printed an edition of Pindar and of the Homeric Scholia, but it did not survive for long.

However, Leo's College of Greeks is neither in its origins nor in its intentions a foundation to promote the study of the Greek Classics in a humanist spirit. Rather it is an echo of the Council of Florence (1439), and of the belated and ephemeral movement to reunite the Church of Constantinople with that of Rome. Its spiritual ancestor is the great Platonist Cardinal Bessarion, one of the few Greeks to take the official adoption of the Roman Catholic creed seriously. The function of Leo's College of Greeks was to collect young Greek pupils from what was by then the Ottoman Empire and to bring them up as Catholics and as missionaries.

The desire to preach the Gospel to the infidels, among whom the schismatic Greeks were perhaps the most execrated, was the motive of the persistent interest of the Franciscan Order in the possibility of linguistic studies for its members. It is due to the Franciscans, and especially to the Catalan friar Ramon Lull, that the Council of Vienne in 1311 issued its decree that teachers of Greek, Hebrew, Arabic and Chaldaean were to be installed and endowed in every university of Christendom.* Although this famous decretal practically remained a dead letter and, beyond a few isolated mentions of converted Jews teaching Hebrew in Paris or Oxford, hardly any palpable traces of its being applied can be found in the next two centuries, it still remains an important factor in the history of Greek studies. For it established the postulate that such philological teaching was part of the duties of a university and it was laid down in the most permanent and conspicuous form imaginable. The decree of Vienne was promulgated as a decretal of Clement V and we know, from Rabelais at least, if not from other sources, that the volume of decretals was held in greater esteem in the universities than the Bible itself, and not a word contained in them could be suppressed or forgotten.

A Franciscan friar Francisco Ximenez de Cisneros (1437–1517) rose to become Archbishop of Toledo, Cardinal and Chancellor of Spain. Disposing of enormous resources, he could single-handed and in a remarkably short time (1498–1508) found and establish an entire new university at Alcala and, within that university a special college, the Collegium Hieronymianum (1516) for the teaching of the three sacred languages: Hebrew, Greek and Latin. With the secured existence of such a college, the aim of the humanist movement was practically achieved, and linguistic training was established as an integral part of university studies. But Spain was then as always somewhat isolated from the rest of Europe, and immediate repercussions of the new foundation are hardly traceable. However, the coincidence that King Francis I of France, as a Spanish prisoner of war after the battle of Pavia, visited Alcala in August 1525, and there was deeply impressed with the modern foundation in being, became a powerful factor in making him upon his return determined to accomplish what he had so long promised to Guillaume Budé and other humanist counsellors, and to found and endow the Collège de France by 1530.*

With the college Ximenez set up the necessary printing office to provide it with books, and the printer, Arnao Guillen de Brocar, brought out his first Greek grammar by 1514 (Chrysoloras, ed. D. Ducas). These energetic Spaniards had by 1514 finished printing the New Testament in Greek under the editorship of the Cretan Demetrios Dukas, and by 1520 the entire Old Testament in Hebrew as well, both with Latin translations. They thereby had attained what was the professed aim of the Erasmian humanists north of the Alps. It is surprising that even after the publication of the whole work, the Complutensian Polyglot Bible, we hear so few repercussions of the great achievement among the scholars of Europe. Considering the preponderant space taken up in the correspondence of Erasmus and his contemporaries by this very question of the original languages and their importance for Biblical studies, references to the Complutensian text or even to its existence are strikingly few. It would seem also from the surviving examples that the number of copies brought from Spain to Northern Europe immediately after publication (1522) was extremely small.

Another country never quite cut off from, but never quite in step with, the rest of Europe is England. Here even in the darker Middle Ages, when no similar phenomenon can be observed on the Continent, there were a few isolated scholars now and then who had a command of Greek. Robert Grosseteste and Roger Bacon in the thirteenth century come to mind most readily; perhaps the dynastic connection with Norman Sicily provides the explanation. Even in the sluggish fifteenth century some Englishmen acquired a knowledge of Greek from the teachers in Italy, such as John Free (d. 1465) and William Selling, who died in 1495.* It is surely significant that in 1525, when the Aldine Press completed its five-volume editio princeps of Galen, the printer Francesco d'Asola mentions in his preface that as press correctors he had enlisted the help of four Englishmen and one German. Of the former, Thomas Lupset and John Clement had their roots in Cambridge and Oxford and their connection with Erasmus and More.*

It is therefore perhaps not so surprising that the introduction of Greek teaching into the two English universities took place so early, and on the whole caused so little friction.* John Fisher, bishop of Rochester and Chancellor of Cambridge, as the adviser and testamentary executor of Lady Margaret Beaufort, founded Christ's College in 1505, St John's in 1511, and in their Statutes laid down an obligation to provide classical teaching. It was Fisher also who, in the summer of 1511, brought Erasmus to Cambridge as our first Greek reader.

At Oxford, where Cardinal Wolsey was the powerful patron of Greek studies and Bishop Richard Fox founded his 'Trilingue' as Corpus Christi College in 1517, we get a little more evidence of traditionalist opposition to the new fashion. The anti-Greek party there even acquired a nickname: the Trojans. Thomas More wrote his letter to Oxford university against the Trojans from Abingdon in 1518.

31

A significant story is told by Erasmus in the letter cited above.* Some theologian preached before Henry VIII and violently attacked Greek studies and the new-fangled translations. Both Thomas More and Richard Pace were present. Henry smiled at them and when the sermon was finished called the preacher before him and asked him if he had ever read Erasmus' writings. The preacher admitted that he had not, and begged the king's pardon. 'Then you are a foolish fellow', said Henry, 'to condemn what you have never read.' He was forbidden ever to preach at court again.

In this atmosphere at court, where Wolsey, More and Pace were at the height of their power, Greek was a fashionable hobby, and the rigid Thomists and Scotists in the universities had to keep rather quiet about it, if they did not want to compromise the chances of preferment for their pupils.

In the Continental countries north of the Alps, the spiritual climate in the chief seats of learning had for long been totally different from that of Italy. For more than two centuries the Church upheld the exclusive right of Paris to teach theology, and when with the Schism the monopoly was broken, the right to establish theological faculties was only grudgingly granted to some, not to all, universities whether old or new. About 1500 a few only of the Italian universities gave degrees in divinity and the newly added theological faculties never gained a preponderant importance.* Bologna remained a school for lawyers, Padua a university for physicians and scientists.

On the teaching of Greek in Paris itself I prefer to speak in my next lecture in connection with the beginnings of Greek printing there. For the present all I wish to say is that what sporadic Greek teaching there was in Paris before the foundation of the Lecteurs Royaux in 1530, generally was given by outsiders and without official sanction from the university authorities; and that the change from cool indifference to violent opposition of the Paris theologians to humanist teaching of any kind does not set in till after the emergence of Lutheranism, and the confusion of philological interest in the Scriptures with the heretical tendencies of the age.

In the universities of Germany and the Netherlands—all founded after 1360 and on the Paris model—the theological faculties maintained their ascendancy from the start. All teaching was subordinate to the ultimate goal of a theological degree, and the Faculty of Arts was hardly more than a preparatory course for the very young students entering college at the age of fifteen or thereabouts.

When the new humanist conceptions of learning, based on eloquence rather than on logic, began to attract the younger generation in the northern universities, they did not find as smooth a passage as in Italy, Spain, or in England, where the foundations of Pope Leo, Ximenez, Fisher, and of Fox paved the way for them. The conservative theological authorities, who strictly controlled Louvain, Cologne, Erfurt and Leipzig, did not countenance the pretentions of the humanists to be accepted as regular lecturers in the Faculty of Arts; for their teaching did not in the least accord with the officially held views on the proper function of the Arts course as a preparation for theological students. Hence the bitter and passionate battles that accompanied the foundation of the Collegium Trilingue at Louvain, the expulsion of the 'poet' Rhagius Aesticampianus from Leipzig in 1511, and the fierce fight against Reuchlin led by the Cologne theologians and its amusing sequel, the *Epistolae Obscurorum Virorum*.

It must be admitted that most of the noisy protagonists of the 'Poetae' could hardly be held in great respect, either for their behaviour as members of the academic body or as men of sound learning. The serious scholars like Reuchlin or Erasmus rather kept away from the stagnating universities. But there were a number of wandering 'poetae', mostly Italian, and mostly disreputable characters, who migrated from one university to another, clamouring for recognition as teachers of eloquence and of the classical authors, such as Girolamo Balbi and Fausto Andrelini at Paris, Richardus Sbrulius and Conrad Celtis in Germany. Their pretentions to true scholarship were of the most hollow, their arrogant attacks on the barbarism of the scholastic dialecticians extremely offensive. But the future was on their side, so to speak, and the younger generation flocked to their lectures and willingly adopted the 'modern' conception of studies based, not on logic chopping, but on an acquaintance with the classical authors and the attainment of an elegant Latin style.

Among the 'slogans' proclaimed by these humanist disciples, the demand for Greek was always in the forefront. But a real knowledge of Greek was extremely rare among them. About 1500 it was still very difficult indeed to obtain a competent teacher of Greek anywhere in the north; witness the long and on the whole, unsuccessful endeavours of the Collegium Trilingue at Louvain to get a first-rate Greek scholar for their professorship, although it carried twice the endowment of the other chairs. The insistence on Greek was a banner waved, a programmatic challenge, rather than a genuine demand for instruction.

Let us follow Richard Croke on his peregrinations through the northern universities and see what he found there. After Eton and King's, after Greek lessons from Grocyn in London, from Erasmus in Cambridge (1510), from Aleander in Paris (1511–12), Croke, still a young man of about twenty three and a B.A., arrived at Louvain and was hospitably received by Jean Desmarais (Paludanus), professor of poetry and of rhetoric. Erasmus himself had lived in his house (1502–4) and dedicated to him his translation of Lucian's *De Mercede Conductis*. The first edition of More's *Utopia*, printed at Louvain in 1516, begins with a commendatory letter from Paludanus to Peter Gillis of Antwerp. Whether Croke really taught Greek at Louvain, as he claims to have done, we cannot prove. If he did, it must have been a very unofficial course of instruction. He moved on to Cologne in 1514.

The two years Croke spent at Louvain were a singularly tranquil period in the story of the establishment of humanistic studies in that university, a lull before the storm. We possess now a very elaborate and excellent study of the early phase of Humanism at Louvain: H. de Vocht's *History of the Foundation of the Collegium Trilingue Lovaniense* (Louvain, 1951). From this we can gather with all the documentary evidence available that an unbroken succession of Italian lecturers read the Classics at Louvain: Raymondo Marliano (1461–75), whose Index Urbium is appended to many early editions of Julius Caesar, Lodovico Bruni (1477–86), Cornelio Vitelli (1487–9), who had been the first to teach Greek at New College, Oxford in 1482–3.

It was in this peaceful and friendly atmosphere of the later fifteenth century that Louvain instilled the love of the classical languages and of the 'Devotio Moderna', the non-scholastic theology based on St Augustine and the Bible, into her pupils. The Frisian Rudolph Agricola, who took his M.A. at Louvain under Marliano in 1465, went on to Italy and became ultimately the first officially appointed academic lecturer in Greek north of the Alps, at Heidelberg, where he died 1485. Richard Fox, bishop of Durham and of Winchester, studied at Louvain in 1479,* and if his foundation of Corpus Christi College, Oxford (1517) so closely resembles the Collegium Trilingue at Louvain, one of the reasons may be that Jerome de Busleiden and Fox formed their ideas on education in the same academy and under the same teachers.

Exotic professors of poetry and of rhetoric reading in the faculty of Arts had been tolerated for a long time by the Louvain authorities. But when in August 1517 Jerome de Busleiden died, and his will called the Collegium Trilingue into being, the traditionalists were faced with a very different problem. Erasmus hurried to Louvain to give the executors of his friend all the help and advice in his power and stayed there till 1521, to see the new foundation through its initial troubles, which he clearly foresaw—four years of fearsome fighting, of every imaginable malice unleashed, of unrelenting opposition from the theologians and their partisans in the Faculty of Arts. The insistence on the 'sacred languages' and especially on Greek, which could only lead to heresy, as Erasmus' New Testament had just proved to them, was the principal stumbling block. Formally the stipulation that the lecturers of the Collegium Trilingue were to be appointed by Busleiden's executors and not by the faculty appeared an intolerable infringement of their privileges, and on that point the university authorities ultimately won. In his endeavours to see Busleiden's College come to life such as he himself had dreamt it, Erasmus was hampered as much by his over-zealous friends as by its frank opponents. Especially some tactless Germans embittered the quarrel with their writings, such as William Nesen whose *Dialogus Bilinguium ac Trilinguium* (printed in 1519) was quite funny in its way, but not conducive to good tempers. In fact it was from Germany and from the turn which matters had taken there that the true virulence was imported into the Louvain struggle. Let us see what situation Richard Croke met at Cologne when he arrived there in 1514.

There is, to the best of my knowledge, no evidence at all for any humanist teaching in Cologne before 1500; the university was strictly controlled by the theologians and in particular by the Dominican Friars, the most rigid guardians of the traditions established by Thomas Aquinas and Albertus Magnus. It is true that Jo. Caesarius of Jülich (1468–1550), who had learned Greek at Bologna, set up as a teacher of Greek at Cologne in 1511, but this was entirely a private undertaking and without any connection whatsoever with the university. Caesarius, a good friend of

Erasmus, had a number of distinguished pupils: Glareanus, Listrius, Cornelius Agrippa, Bullinger, Mosellanus (who became Croke's successor at Leipzig), etc., learned their Greek from him.*

After a preliminary skirmish between the Dominican Inquisitor Jacobus van Hoogstraeten and an Italian teacher of Roman Law, Peter Tomai of Ravenna, in 1506–8,* the battle between the Cologne theologians and the humanists broke out in its full fury, and with world-shaking repercussions. The 'Battle of the Jewish Books' began in 1509 when an over-zealous Jewish convert, John Pfefferkorn, demanded the confiscation and destruction of all Hebrew books, and the Cologne authorities were willing to back him. The eminent scholar and Hebraist John Reuchlin (1455–1522) wrote against this proposal, and there started a battle of pamphlets of unheard of violence, as well as legal proceedings carried even before the Emperor and the Pope himself.* From an antisemitic outburst the quarrel rose to the level of an urgent defence of all philological studies. Practically all the humanistically minded scholars of Europe, Erasmus at their head, rallied in support of Reuchlin and, while the prosecution was still in suspense in the Roman Curia, his friends brought out a volume of attestations to his piety and his scholarly eminence, the *Epistolae Clarorum Virorum* (Tübingen, 1514).

Reuchlin was left in peace. The indignant support of the whole world of letters proved an efficient protection. But very soon the literary efforts in his defence were switched into a much more powerful attack on the Cologne reactionaries. The *Epistolae Clarorum Virorum* were followed in autumn 1515 by the *Epistolae Obscurorum Virorum*. Never perhaps in history has a witty satirical pamphlet come nearer to proving the truth of the saying that ridicule can kill. The forty-one letters in grotesque German dog Latin, professing to be addressed to Ortwin Gratius, a well-known Cologne university teacher, issued anonymously and under a false imprint from the press of Heinrich Gran at Hagenau in Alsace.* They had been concocted at a merry supper table at Erfurt where Mutianus Rufus, Hermann von dem Busch and Crotus Rubianus used to foregather.

Let us have a specimen; a letter from a Leipzig Bachelor of Arts:

Reverend Herr Magister! You must know that there is a notable question here that I desire, or entreat, to be by you magistrally determined.

There is a certain Grecian here who readeth in Urban's grammar, and whenever he writeth Greek he always putteth tittles atop.

Thereupon I said, a little while ago, 'Magister Ortwin of Deventer also handleth Greek grammar, and he is as well qualified therein as that fellow, and yet he never maketh tittles so; and I trow he knoweth his business as well as that Grecian—ay, and can put him to rights'. Nevertheless some distrusted me in this matter, wherefore my friends and fellow-students besought me to write to your worthiness so that you might make it known to me whether we ought to put tittles or no. And if we ought not to put them, then by the Lord, we will roundly harry that Grecian and bring it to pass that his hearers shall be but few.

Of a truth I took note of you at Cologne, in Heinrich Quentell's house, when you were reader and had to correct Greek, that you would strike out all the tittles that were above the letters and say: 'Of what use are these fiddle-faddles?' And it hath just come into my mind that you must have had some ground for this or you would not have done it.*

This 'Grecian who put the tittles atop' is surely Richard Croke, who had come from Cologne to Leipzig before the end of the year 1514. About a year later than the first edition, but certainly by 1517, there comes a second part of the *Epistolae Obscurorum Virorum* of which the (anonymous) author is undoubtedly Ulrich von Hutten; somewhat more bitter, a little less funny, but still not an unworthy sequel. Here we have another letter from Leipzig: 'There is also another here who lectures on Greek, Richard Croke by name, and he comes from England. And just now I said: Does he come from England? The devil he does. I truly believe if there were a poet where the pepper grows, he would also come to Leipzig.'*

The *Epistolae Obscurorum Virorum*, fictitious and malevolent though they may be, do give a vivid picture of the hostility of the Leipzig university authorities towards all humanistic instruction. What is surprising is that this attitude had persisted unchanged for so long, that attempts to teach the Classics and eloquence had been made repeatedly ever since the sixties of the fifteenth century, and that they had mostly ended quickly enough with the expulsion of the 'poetae' in question. We have a very thorough study of the subject in G. Bauch, *Geschichte des Leipziger Frühhumanismus* (Leipzig, 1899) (XXII. *Beiheft zum Centralblatt für Bibliothekswesen*). Here we can read that the Florentine humanist Jacobus Publicius lectured there as early as 1467,* and soon went on to more congenial climates. Conrad Celtis, the German 'Arch-Humanist', appears as a lecturer at Leipzig in 1486, publishes his *Ars Versificandi et Carminum* there, and begins to edit

Seneca's tragedies one by one. By 1487 the Leipzig authorities expelled him. On the protracted war of pamphlets (1500–3) between the humanist physician Martin of Mellerstadt and the theologian Conrad Wimpina on the merits of poetic studies, Bauch informs us in far too tedious detail. In 1508 a more serious 'poeta laureatus', the Silesian Johannes Rhagius Aesticampianus (who knew Greek), begins to lecture at Leipzig, cautiously stressing the literary merits of St Jerome, St Augustine and other fathers of the Church rather than of the pagan poets. After pocketing the insults and humiliations of the doctors and magistri of the superior faculties for three years, and having persistently been refused a lecture-room for his new-fangled course of poetry and classical grammar, Rhagius left of his own accord in 1511. His farewell speech, recounting his grievances and defending the poetic discipline, a most interesting and significant document, was printed at Speyer; because of this speech the Leipzig authorities rusticated the departed poet for ten years.

Not until 1519, and then by the energetic intervention of George Duke of Saxony, Erasmus' personal friend, was the long-lasting enmity of the Leipzig faculties overcome, and humanist teaching was given its recognised place. In 1519 also the university bought the Greek Aristotle for its library, while as recently as 1515 they still had insisted on the old medieval translations of Aristotle for the basis of their teaching, and had banned the Renaissance versions.

Beyond any doubt it was Richard Croke, the newly appointed Greek lecturer, who was the principal driving spirit behind the venture of Siberch's press. No doubt either that Croke really knew Greek and really wished to teach it. Let us not forget however that he came to Cambridge straight from Leipzig, where during three full years he had enjoyed the exhilarating experience of the battle between 'obscuri viri' and 'poetae' at its fiercest. The programmatic fulminations of humanists and Aristotelians against each other, with the help of the printing press, were to him an essential and enlivening element of academic activity. The gradual infiltration of linguistic teaching, such as Fisher and his protégé Erasmus had so successfully initiated it, avoided friction as far as possible, but to Croke and his more ardent disciples it seemed much too slow. A bold attack on the crusty old obstructionist dons by means of a succession of pamphlets was called for. In the calmer atmosphere of Cambridge these tactics fell flat. Nobody seems to have become terribly excited, even about the *Hermathena*, and no theological pens hastened to defend tradition by a stunning reply.

Between 1518, when Croke had left Leipzig, and 1521 when Siberch began printing, times had greatly changed. What had been a purely academic quarrel about barbarous Latin and the Defence of Poesy, carried on with zest and gusto but without involving the deepest emotions, was now becoming entangled with fierce religious controversy. The fight against the theologians, because they spoke and wrote such awful Latin, turned into an attack upon the theology they were teaching. In July 1519, when Croke delivered his speech in Cambridge in praise of Greek studies, the disputation was in full swing at Leipzig.* In 1520 Luther was excommunicated, in 1521 his books were burned in London. The anti-theologians had to decide for themselves whether they would shift their opposition to the new ground or bury, for the time being at least, their aesthetic animosities and rally to the cause of preserving the unity of the Church. Few of them, like Erasmus, chose the latter course, the majority of the northern humanists turned Protestant.

Anti-clericalism was no longer a demand for a better educated and more respectable clergy, it had become a pretty dangerous attitude in most countries outside Northern Germany. Many people besides Erasmus himself regretted some of the less restrained pieces they had published; they were liable to be misinterpreted as significant for their doctrinal position. Our own generation is witnessing a very similar shift of opinion. Chronologically speaking the last infirmity of noble minds was an admiring sympathy with the Russian revolution, and not only in America are there now many who would rather see forgotten what they said or wrote in the 1930's.

By 1522 the gay anti-barbarous humanists had become very silent and Siberch's press closed down. Nowadays not only Bullock, Pace and Croke, but also the Continental 'poetae', so vociferous about 1500, are completely forgotten, and nobody reads the Odes and Orations by which they expected to immortalise their names and those of their patrons. They were with very few exceptions clumsy poets and mediocre scholars. Their best achievements, and the only ones that can still be read with pleasure, are their programmatic utterances: Pace's *De Fructu qui ex Doctrina Percipitur* or Busch's *Vallum Humanitatis*, or Budé's *De Studio Literarum*, are spirited formulations of the humanist ideals which they themselves never attained. As individual authors they have rightly passed into oblivion, but did they leave no mark on European literature that makes their intense dedication to 'good letters' worth remembering?

Their enduring achievement lies in a direction they never aimed at and never foresaw: they created 'grammar' and 'prose-style' for all the living languages. The word 'style' is a European word first used by Quintilian in the sense we understand it now. The Middle Ages did not know the word or the conception. The humanists revived the postulate of stylistic elegance and of syntactic 'concinnitas'. If Francis Bacon by the end of the century wrote English prose, it is because the humanists imposed the fundamental rules of Latin grammar on the uncouth vernacular such as Caxton wrote it.

There was no such thing as English, French or German grammar. From the struggle of humanistically trained schoolmasters with a recalcitrant vulgar speech there emerges the prose of all modern languages.

III

CONTINENTAL SCHOLAR-PRINTERS

S IBERCH started printing with a fount of roman type obviously
brand new, for it is singularly sharp and clear in his earliest impressions and it soon gets visibly blunted and less brilliant. It is an elegant
slender tall roman of which few distinctive characteristics could be described in words, except one curious feature which I have never seen in
any other type: his lower-case 'g' has no 'ear' on the right at all.

Where did Siberch, who came from Cologne, obtain his type? Certainly from Germany. Ferguson has shown that he brought some of his
woodcuts and ornaments from Cologne.* So it appears, as a first guess,
that the type also might come from there. But no similar type is used by
any Cologne printer.

Although it is not possible to find an exact duplicate of Siberch's type
anywhere, it is in many respects extremely similar to certain roman types
employed at Erfurt, at Wittenberg, at Leipzig and at Vienna, a design
which Proctor in his classification of types has named the Leipzig-Erfurt
style and in particular the 'Sertorius variety'.* These types share many
characteristics of Siberch's fount.

The earliest appearance of such a type is met with at Erfurt at a press
started and financed by a remarkable man, Nicolaus Marschalk of
Thuringia, hence 'Thurius'. Throughout his career (he died at Rostock
in 1525) he was an ardent and remarkably well-read Greek scholar and
also, wherever he taught, a venturesome and successful patron of printing.*
Marschalk first emerges as a humanist lecturer in the university of Erfurt*
in 1499, when he brings out an edition of a treatise on diet by the
Byzantine scholar Psellus from the press of Wolfgang Schenk. It is in
Latin, but Marschalk's commentary gives several passages in Greek
printed in a primitive Greek type without accents, which may well be
the earliest Greek type cut in Germany, or in Northern Germany at any
rate.*

Marschalk soon relinquished his dependence on Wolfgang Schenk as
a printer and started his own private press with a new roman type, which is
the one closely resembling Siberch's type, and a new Greek type as well.

With this fresh equipment he published on 1 October 1501 a Hesiod, *Laus Musarum ex Theogonia*, which has a colophon announcing that it was printed by one Henricus Sertorius. In 1502 Marschalk migrated to Wittenberg taking his two types with him. In 1507 he wandered on to Rostock, where again he started a press with the same roman type, active by 1514 if not before. In view of all this, I would have preferred to call this roman type 'Marschalk type', but Proctor is, as always, being precise and consistent, and since the type first appeared in a book signed by one Sertorius (who is never heard of again), he calls it 'Sertorius type', and so it must remain. Among Marschalk's other publications at Erfurt, presumably with Sertorius as his press man, there is an astonishing book called *Enchiridion Poetarum*, April 1502 (Proctor 11231), a big quarto of no less than 462 leaves, an anthology of excerpts from the Classical and Renaissance poets, with woodcut portraits of Virgil, Sappho and other authors, including Marschalk himself.

In 1502 the Duke of Saxony founded a university at Wittenberg, soon to attain world-wide celebrity because of Luther's theses announced for disputation in a broadside nailed to a church door. Marschalk at once joined the new faculty as the 'poet' and public orator, and set up a press with the equipment he brought from Erfurt. His printer-craftsman there was not Sertorius, as Proctor assumed because of the identity of the type,* but Hermannus Trebelius, a countryman of Marschalk's from Thuringia, and soon to become noted as a Latin poet in his own right. His name does not happen to be found in either of the two specimens of this press in the British Museum, but there exists a Wittenberg impression signed by him in 1504.*

Marschalk started his press, the first to operate in Wittenberg, with a little quarto of ten leaves (Proctor 11826), completed on 1 February 1503: *Oratio habita a N. M. T. Albiori Academia in Alemannia superiori ad promotionem primorum Baccalauriorum*, with the colophon: 'Impressum Albiori. Kal. Feb. 1503.' In this university oration Marschalk, after a discourse on laurels and crowns and other prizes, goes on to tell of the Judgement of Paris. On p. 9 we read: 'Apud Lucianum philosophum in Paridis Judicio ita Mercurius a Jove missus inquit: σε ὦ Παρὶ κελεύω'... and so on, in Greek. The promises of the three goddesses to Paris are equally cited verbatim in Greek. The Judgement of Paris is the twentieth of Lucian's *Dialogues of the Gods*, and though the legend, which is not found in Homer, was well known to medieval writers and artists, it is from Lucian that the Renaissance period mainly derives its knowledge of it.

The first product of the printing press in a university town, a type closely resembling Siberch's, the ostentatious employment of Greek type, an oration held at a solemn university ceremony and a translation of Lucian, surely these five points suggest a striking similarity to Cambridge and to Bullock, his *Oration* and his Lucian.

But before we can generalise on the literary characteristics of the early academic presses we must extend our survey over other university towns. The next is Frankfurt on the Oder, where a university was founded in 1506 by Joachim, Margrave of Brandenburg. Among the first members to be matriculated we find three printers: Conrad Baumgart (who came from Breslau), Johannes Jamer de Hanau and Balthasar Murrer from Basle. Among Baumgart's earliest publications in 1507, there is an oration by the young 'Poeta' Publius Vigilantius, *Ad Joachimum Brandenburgensem Franckfordianae Urbis ad Oderam et Gymnasii Literarii Introductionis Ceremoniarumque Observationum Descriptio*. This is the speech delivered by the twenty-year-old Strassburg 'poeta et orator' at the inthronisation ceremony inaugurating the university on 26 April 1506. Six years later Vigilantius set out for Italy to learn Greek, and was murdered by highwaymen on the road. The sense of loss among his friends at Frankfurt was profound, and the poet-printer Hermannus Trebelius composed an elegy on his death, *Nenia Hermanni Trebelii in Obitu...Publii Vigilantii Poete*. This was printed in 1512 by Johannes Jamer de Hanau, who adds in the end the significant sentence: 'Hec pro amore defuncti Joannes Hanauius non Gothicis sed Romanis literis excussit.'*

Nicolaus Marschalk left Wittenberg in 1507, taking his types with him, and went to Rostock, where a small university existed since 1419, and printing presses had been intermittently at work since 1476. There he became a counsellor of the Duke of Mecklenburg and obviously a man of some affluence. For when he started his press again, by 1514 at the latest, he could afford to print practically only his own writings, and these in magnificent style with plentiful woodcut illustrations. His book on state affairs, civil and military, 1515, has over a hundred cuts of engines of war, copied from an Erfurt 1511 Vegetius; his book on fishes and sea-monsters, 1517, is equally well illustrated. Both contain numerous quotations in Greek. His big history of Mecklenburg, *Annales Herulorum et Vandalorum*,

1521, I have never seen. But Marschalk's Rostock productions, however remarkable and learned, hardly come within the definition of an 'academic press'; they are rather the output of a rich man's private printing establishment.*

However, as we pointed out above (p. 38), it was from Leipzig that Richard Croke, the principal initiator of Siberch's press, came to Cambridge, it was at Leipzig that he first saw his *Rudimenta Graeca* in print, and it is to Leipzig that we must now turn to see what specimens of humanist printing it can offer. We have shown that Leipzig was the most determined opponent of humanism among all universities, and we are not surprised to find that no roman type is used there at all before 1511. The humanist publications of Celtis, of Polich von Mellerstadt, of Rhagius Aesticampianus, that issue from Leipzig presses are all printed in Gothic characters. Melchior Lotter is the first Leipzig printer to own a roman type, and he is proud indeed of his up-to-date equipment; in the colophons of his impressions in that type he calls attention to the 'novae formae' in 1511, to his 'venustiores typi' in 1513. It is a tall narrow roman 'like Sertorius 1', says Proctor. Practically the same fount is used by Jacob Thanner and by Valentin Schumann (who printed Croke's *Tabulae* but not in this type in 1516). When we find three Leipzig printers simultaneously using a type so similar in design to Siberch's, it becomes very likely that it is from a Leipzig typefounder that Croke advised Siberch to obtain his types.

A brief glance at some of the titles that issue in these new characters. The first, in 1511, is a translation from the Greek: Libanius, *De Uxore Loquaci*, by an otherwise unknown Wigand von Salza. In 1513 Lotter prints a selection of Lucian's *Dialogues*, in Latin of course, edited by the Leipzig humanist Veit Werler, and Philip Melanchthon's translation of Lucian's *Calumnia* in 1518. Lucian, you will see, is practically an obligatory hallmark for these humanist presses. The *Polixena* of Leonardo Bruni Aretino and a Persius follow later, but from 1518 onwards Lotter became wholly absorbed with printing Luther's writings, and his son, Melchior Lotter the younger, transferred the press to Wittenberg. Jacob Thanner prints Poliziano, Sabellico and Horace in this type as well as Reuchlin's Latin school plays. Valentin Schumann in 1515 brings out Richard Croke's edition of Ausonius, and in 1518 Petrus Mosellanus' translation of Lucian's *Charon* and *Tyrannus*.

Two other eastern university towns have to be mentioned here in which roman type similar to the 'Sertorius variety' appears in humanist publications. From Cracow in Poland we get as early as 1504 a Libanius: *Epistolae* translated from the Greek by the Italian humanist Francesco Zambeccari, and here edited by the same Jo. Rhagius Aesticampianus whom we encountered as an exasperating 'poeta' ejected by the Leipzig reactionaries in 1511. This Libanius is printed for the Cracow publisher Jo. Haller by one Joannes Clymes, who is never heard of again, nor does the type ever reappear. Much closer to the Sertorius type is that which Hieronymus Vietor brought with him from Vienna to Cracow by 1518, and which he used to print a description of the wedding festivities of King Sigismund of Poland, also a Cebes, *Tabula*, and other humanistic texts.

Vietor, a Silesian by birth, sometimes alone, sometimes with his partner Singriener, had employed his Sertorius roman at Vienna ever since 1510, bringing out an impressive series of humanist and classical books. On Vienna sixteenth-century printing we are particularly well informed, because we possess Michael Denis' *Wiens Buchdruckergeschichte bis 1560* (Vienna, 1782; with Supplement, 1793), which to my mind remains the unsurpassed model of what such a monograph on local typographical history can and should be. To each of the 832 items he describes, Denis has added a note on the author, the recipient of the dedication and all other contributors to the book, so that his annotation provides an admirable survey of intellectual and scholarly life in Vienna from 1482 to 1560.

Under the Emperor Maximilian I (1493–1519), imaginative though inefficient, display-loving though permanently in money difficulties, there was quite a notable faction of humanist scholars and 'poetae' in Vienna University, which he encouraged and protected, though he would reward them with cheap laurel crowns rather than with bags of gold. Austrian, Italian, German and Swiss humanists read the Classics and wrote laudatory verses to each other. The earliest and most famous of them, Conrad Celtis, had died in 1508. In the nine years (1510–18) of Vietor's principal activity as an academic printer in roman letters, the most eminent scholars who kept his press busy with their writings and editions were Joachim Vadianus of St Gall in Switzerland and Joannes Camers, an Italian Giovanni Ricuzzi of Camerino.*

It is not possible to give anything like an enumeration of the remarkable books that issued from this press, but I cannot refrain from citing a few of the most interesting. Erasmus' translation of Euripides, together with his *De Laudibus Britanniae* and the *Ode to Henry VII* was reprinted from the Aldine edition of 1507; also Linacre's translation of Proclus from the Aldine of 1499. Both of these were seen through the press by Vadianus in 1511. Reuchlin's translation of the Homeric *Battle of Frogs and Mice* followed in 1516. A first edition of a medieval poem, Walafrid Strabo's *Hortulus* (1510), is notable because it also contains some verses by the Anglo-Saxon Aldhelm, his first appearance in print. Many Classical authors, Claudian, Florus, Cicero of course, the *Panegyrici*, Diodorus Siculus in Latin, and others followed year by year. The inevitable *Dialogues* of Lucian in a translation by Brassicanus did not appear till 1527 from Singriener's press. Many of these books contained Greek passages, but there is none printed entirely in Greek.

We have so far followed a purely typographic clue, the Sertorius roman, which has led us, rather surprisingly, to a group of university towns at the opposite end of Europe viewed from Cambridge. But note that my survey is to the best of my knowledge a comprehensive one; no Sertorius type is met outside these five towns, and they are all university towns. There are other striking analogies between these presses. They were all at work in predominantly 'scholastic' universities, and each one can be said to have been run by an identifiable group of humanist scholars acting in opposition to the majority opinion of the higher faculties. They proudly used their new roman type to proclaim their advanced taste and their abhorrence of all Gothic barbarism. They all made a point of inserting some words or passages in Greek letters, which hardly anybody in their vicinity could read or even decipher.

The texts these presses chose to print also show many similarities. Speeches held on ceremonial occasions, translations of short pieces from the Greek, some compositions by the Italian humanists, all such small pamphlets cannot have been printed with an eye on profit; they must have been financed by the humanist enthusiasts backing the printer.

We observe a certain community of outlook and of taste in these five, or, with Cambridge, six local groups, which not only made them concur in preferring the Sertorius roman as the most elegant type available, but went much further than that in literary and scholarly predilections.

Let us abandon now the confining link of type-design, which has taken us to such unexpected spiritual kindred in the East. It is obvious that

Erfurt and Cracow, as well as Cambridge, did not originate the fashions they shared, they merely reflected a powerful impulse stemming from the greater centres of cultural activity in Italy and in France. Cambridge and Leipzig in the first quarter of the sixteenth century were equally peripheral when seen from Rome or Paris. It is time to turn to the much more important humanist presses in Western Europe, which serve the same tendencies in a far more advanced stage of development.

We have already glanced at the bold achievement of Ximenez at Alcala, of which we find no echo beyond the Pyrenees, and also at the short-lived Greek press which Leo X established at Rome. We do not propose to revert to these printing centres (although a good deal more might be said about Rome), and we now approach the vast and complicated subject of Paris.

It would be quite hopeless to attempt a brief sketch of Paris humanist teaching and printing, were it not that we possess on that subject the most admirable book by A. Renaudet, *Préréforme et Humanisme à Paris, 1494–1517* (Paris, 1916), to which I must refer you for an account of the wider ideological conflicts and for many details.* Renaudet gives an exposition of the interplay of intellectual movements in the university with the political struggles of the Gallican Church against the Papacy, he stresses the predominance of the general anxiety for Church and monastic Reform colouring both humanist and traditionalist thought, and he achieves a narrative that is lucid and readable. Moreover, for our purposes Renaudet's book is quite exceptional among historical studies in that he bases his account very largely on an exact examination of the books printed at Paris between 1494 and 1517, their prefaces, their dedications and their contents. It is therefore possible for me to beg you to read Renaudet if you wish to gain an insight into the spiritual and intellectual background of the scholars and printers I am going to cite. Postulating an acquaintance with Renaudet, I can skip the early humanists like Balbi, Andrelini, Gaguin, etc., and the earliest Greek teachers like Gregorius Tifernas (1458), and that Georgius Hermonymus of Sparta from whom Erasmus tried in vain to get much help in his passionate desire for Greek studies (1501).*

The Paris book-trade in the first quarter of the sixteenth century is a far more numerous and varied organisation than that of the comparatively provincial towns we have dealt with so far. To distinguish peculiarly 'academic presses' is impossible because the entire book-trade was, since long before the days of printing, a limb and branch of Paris University subject to regulation by the Masters and, more directly, by the 'Libraires jurés de l'Université'. The foremost among them was Jean Petit (1492–1530), who dominates the Paris book-market with his innumerable publications, printed by himself or by many other printers for him; a publishing *œuvre* much too varied to permit of any characterisation.

A striking fact when we survey the presses before 1525 is the high percentage of aliens working in the Paris trade, not quite as dominant as in England, but still amounting to more than half of the persons employed. They were mainly Flemings, Germans and Swiss; Denys Roce was a Scotsman.

One of these Flemings, Jodocus Badius van Assche of Ghent* becomes the most prominent of the humanist Paris printers; more than that, his attainments as a scholar, as a Latin stylist and his familiarity with Greek made him, next to Budé and Lefèvre d'Étaples, the leading light of the 'modern' literary movement in France. When Erasmus in his *Ciceronianus* (1528) gave offence to the chauvinistic French by placing Badius as a writer of Latin in the same rank as, if not above, Budé and any other Paris humanist, he may have been less than tactful, but he uttered a sincere and defensible opinion.

Badius came to Paris in 1499 after studying at Louvain and Bologna and after some years at Lyons in Trechsel's office as a printer. In 1503 he starts his Paris press, the Prelum Ascensianum. It was not long, April 1505, before he brought out one of the momentous books of the century, Valla's *Annotations on the New Testament*, written about 1440, which Erasmus had just discovered in the library of the abbey du Parc outside Louvain, a work that determined Erasmus' own dedication to biblical studies and directly led to his Greek Testament of 1516.* In the following year, 1506, we get from Badius' press the two plays of Euripides in Erasmus' version dedicated to Archbishop Warham, and in the same year Lucian's *Dialogues* translated partly by Erasmus, partly by Thomas More. In 1512 there follows the first edition of Erasmus' *De duplici Copia*.

However it is not sufficient to point to a few Erasmus first editions and thereupon to declare Badius a great humanist printer. What is needed is to cast a glance at the titles of his total output of over 700 volumes which Renouard has so conveniently listed in chronological order on pp. 71–103 of his first volume. The most rapid survey will show that the proportion of ancient classics and humanist compositions constitutes about nine-tenths of Badius' *œuvre*, and that the residue of strictly scholastic and theological titles is generally undertaken in partnership with some other firm, mostly Jean Petit. That signifies to my mind that Badius accepted the job of printing, but did not care to attend to the distribution of these volumes; his own customers and business connections were wholly specialised in humanist literature.

That Badius published the writings of Guillaume Budé (*Annotationes in Pandectas*, 1508, *De Asse*, 1515), of his own teacher Philippus Beroaldus, of the Italian court-poet Fausto Andrelini, and of most other French humanist poets goes without saying. What is perhaps worth noting is that he did not disdain to include some remarkable medieval books never seen in print before. Geoffrey of Monmouth came out in 1508 and again in 1517, and so did four of Guil. Parvi's first editions of early historians: Gregory of Tours (1512), Liutprand of Cremona (1514), Aimoinus of Fleury (1514), Paulus Diaconus (1514).* Equally unexpected perhaps was the publication in 1511 of the *Dogma Moralium Philosophorum* by the twelfth-century Chartres Platonist Guillaume de Conches. Such medieval exhumations are a characteristic of the humanist printers—witness Siberch's Baldwin of Canterbury or Vietor's Walafrid Strabo.

Erasmus came to Paris in 1495 and his first appearance in print is his admiring letter to Gaguin included in the *Gesta Francorum* of 30 September 1495, very badly printed by Pierre le Dru. Soon after, perhaps by November 1495, we have his first independent publication, the little undated poem *De Casa natalitia Jesu* (GW 9375) from the press of Antoine Denidel. Neither of these printers can be regarded as specialised in humanism. Nor can the German printer John Philippi of Creuznach be so described, to whom fell the honour of issuing the first, very meagre, edition of the *Adagia* in 1500.* In fact it is not easy to point to any of the early sixteenth-century Paris presses outside that of Badius as a definitely humanistic printing establishment; any one of the numerous printers was as likely as not to include a humanistic poem or grammar among their varied output.

There is however one Paris press, that of Gilles de Gourmont,* which makes a bold new departure. In 1507 he starts to print little books entirely in Greek, thereby putting Paris first among any towns outside Italy to embark on the production of text-books needed by intending students of Greek, obviously a rather unprofitable undertaking for quite a few years yet. Aldus' Greek Classics had begun to appear in the Paris bookshops and we know from various sources that they were considered to be outrageously expensive. At the same time war had broken out with Venice and the resulting blockade had forced Aldus to suspend all printing for the entire two years 1506–7. Conditions were favourable for trying the experiment.

Gourmont could not cope with the difficulty of the Greek accents and breathings, or else he tried to economise in an ingenious but inadequate way on the extra variety of punches which Aldus had provided. He tried the expedient of printing the text lines spaced, and between them in a separate line the accents. This was not very satisfactory because it is not easy to make out to which letters exactly the accents belonged. Not till 1512 did Gourmont succeed in mastering the problem.

As an editor for his little Greek text-books he obtained the services of François Tissard of Amboise, who had just returned to Paris from Bologna, where he had spent three years obtaining a law degree and learning Greek from Demetrius of Sparta. Perhaps it would be more correct to say that Tissard obtained the services of Gourmont as a printer of the Greek text-books he needed for the courses he proposed to give. Tissard brought out only four Greek books for Gourmont, all in 1507, and all only reprints of bits and pieces from Aldus' more voluminous publications. They include a Hesiod, *Works and Days*, the Homeric *Battle of Frogs and Mice* and the grammar of Chrysoloras. His fifth book issued in January 1509 is a very curious one, a Hebrew grammar, introduced by a substantial auto-biographic preface in the form of a Lucianic dialogue between 'Prothy-mopatris' and 'Phronimus'. With great display of patriotic concern Tissard expresses his doubts whether it would be wise for him to persist as the first French teacher of Greek and of Hebrew, and whether he would not do better to revert to his law career.

The reasons for these misgivings are quite easy to fathom. The Italian Jerome Aleander* had arrived in Paris in June 1508 with letters of re-commendation from Erasmus (who was then at Venice), and with a con-siderable reputation both as a Greek and a Hebrew scholar. Aldus had dedicated to him his Homer of 1504. Aleander was not only a much better scholar than Tissard, he was also a singularly pushful character, who ended his career as a Cardinal of the Church (1538, died 1542). Under the pro-tection of Guillaume Budé he soon got hold of Tissard's paying pupils and began his public lectures on Greek on 22 April 1509 with great

success; Tissard had abandoned his Greek courses in January 1509.*
Aleander had little difficulty in persuading Gourmont that he would
make a much better editor of his Greek books. From April 1509 (a Plutarch *Opuscula*) until he left Paris for the Netherlands in 1514, Aleander
brought out ten Greek titles, including some *Dialogues* of Lucian and
a remarkable Greek-Latin Dictionary, which is not a mere reprint of
anything published before, though based on the Aldine Crastonus.

After Aleander's departure, Gourmont's Greek press issued another ten
books, edited by various pupils of Aleander's; but after 1517 no more is
heard of it for a long time. Gourmont was by no means only occupied with
his Greek text-books. He printed a good many Latin titles and among them
the first edition of Erasmus' *Praise of Folly* (1511). We know that it was
Richard Croke, then in Paris as Aleander's pupil, who read the proofs of
the *Moria*, not at all to the author's satisfaction.

Before we turn northwards, following Aleander and Croke, we must
glance at the other French universities in the provinces. There were
printing presses at work in several of these towns, but little strictly
'humanist' printing. The prolific presses of Caen* and of Toulouse*
certainly brought out a sprinkling of classics and humanist compositions,
but no printer can be described as specialising in this field. At Valence,
a law university first and foremost, Jean Belon used roman type in 1515
to print Aymar du Rivail's *History of Roman and of Canon Law*. Poitiers*
seems a particularly lively centre at the very end of the fifteenth and in
the first years of the sixteenth century, and although we meet with no
roman type being used there, Claudin describes quite a number of significant titles, such as an elegy on the fall of Constantinople by one Florentin
Liquenay of Tours, the *Ethics* of Aristotle in the Argyropulos translation,
a number of the works of Baptista Mantuanus and several Classics. A
unique Lucian, *Charon*, in Rinuccio's translation, printed by J. Bouhier
and J. Bouchet before 1498, which even Claudin did not know, is in
Cambridge University Library.

However, the most active centre of humanist enthusiasm in France at
the turn of the century, the law university of Orléans, had no printing
press at all. And still we may not pass it over in silence, not only because
it was at Orléans that Erasmus struggled with the Greek Homer in 1500,
and at Orléans that he met his friends Jerome de Busleiden and Nicolas
Bérauld, but mainly because of another pupil and admirer he found there,

John Pyrrhus d'Angleberme. He was the son of an Orléans physician, Peter d'Angleberme, with whom Erasmus was on terms of great friendship; Erasmus tutored the young man on his return to Paris. In 1512, when the plague was again raging at Paris, Jerome Aleander came to lecture at Orléans, and there he composed his rudimentary Greek *Tabulae*, printed the next year for Gilles de Gourmont by Robert de Keysere,* which became so important a tool in elementary Greek teaching. Pyrrhus d'Angleberme had the benefit of Aleander's instruction and later became professor of law and rector in Orléans University. He died at Milan in 1521.*

In 1517 John Pyrrhus d'Angleberme published a volume of very varied content, partly legal, comprising the entire text of the *Costumes d'Orléans*, partly humanistic, including a translation of Lucian on dancing (*De Saltatione*). One of the pieces included is a *Panegyricus Aureliae ubi Locus de Jurisprudentiae Laudibus Egregius*. The book is on the title announced for sale at Orléans in the house of Jacques Hoys, 'vulgariter À l'Escripvainnerie pres l'Eglise Nostre Dame des Bonnes Nouvelles', but, there being no printer at Orléans, it is printed at Paris by André Bocard. The main text of the book is not in roman but in gothic type, although it is heavily interspersed with Greek quotations.

Here we have the full academic humanist pattern, the ceremonial speech in praise of his university, the translation from Lucian and, most interesting of all to us, the dedicatory preface to his patron Louis de Bourbon, bishop of Laon. In this Preface, printed in roman type, we are given the full formulation of the humanistic programme, and the attack on the ignorant theologians who do not know the Fathers of the Church: 'Sed quid accuso Theologos? Quamvis ab eorum albo refixum Hebraice, Graece et Latine perdoctum virum Reuchlinum, etiam indicta causa damnatum, quis est qui non aegre ferat? Hoc Hermolao, Pico, Erasmo, Fabro reliquisque quos ea afficit injuria negotium relinquo.' Two pages further on we find a most striking enumeration of the French humanists active at the time, beginning with Deloynes, Budé, Longueil, Nicolas Bérauld, and adding seven further names of lesser notoriety. Although it is not the product of an 'academic press' I do not see how I could omit all mention of this significant book.

Louvain university was founded by the Duke of Burgundy in 1425, and long before the opening of the Collegium Trilingue in 1517 it held the position 'as one of the earliest and for a time by far the most famous home of the New Learning in Europe'.*

Here at last we find what we have been looking for so far afield: the humanist press entirely devoted to the demands of the 'poets' and rhetoricians, and not only persisting but evidently flourishing through the first thirty years of the sixteenth century. Even the first of the Louvain printers, John Veldener, had published Cicero's *Letters* as early as 1475 (GW 6814) and in 1477 those of Enea Silvio Piccolomini. His rival and successor, John of Westphalia, through the seventies and eighties of the century, proved by the substantial admixture of classical and humanist titles (Virgil, Juvenal, Quintilian, Cicero, Barzizza, etc.) that he knew where to sell the modern type of book. I expect that, apart from Louvain itself and the scholars in the Netherlands, England was quite an important market for him.

But the man who really can be called the humanist printer *par excellence* is Thierry Martens of Alost* who, having begun to print in his home town as early as 1473, moved to Louvain on the news of John of Westphalia's death in 1498. His start there is a strange one: he printed two Breviaries, one for the diocese of Liége, the other for Salisbury. But he soon must have convinced himself that his future did not lie in liturgical printing, and after the turn of the century he devoted himself predominantly to the cause of humanism, first at Antwerp, then from 1512 permanently at Louvain. His titles to fame in that field are too numerous to recite: the first edition of More's *Utopia* (1516) and nearly a dozen Erasmus first editions stand to his credit, including the *Enchiridion Militis Christiani* (1503), the *Institutio Principis Christiani* (1516, published in partnership with Gilles de Gourmont of Paris), and the first two sizeable collections of Erasmus' *Letters* (1516–17). He is the first to print the writings of Rudolphus Agricola (1511, 1515) and of J. L. Vives (1519). Before even the Collegium Trilingue opened its doors, Thierry Martens began to print small Greek text-books for those anxious to learn the language. He started with Aleander's *Tabulae Graecarum Musarum adyta Compendio Ingredi Cupientibus*...in March 1516, such as they had been issued by Gilles de Gourmont in Paris in 1512. His helper in this novel enterprise was Rutger Rescius,* who had been Aleander's pupil at Paris. These rudimentary *Tabulae* were immediately followed by the Greek grammars of Lascaris and of Gaza and by a reprint of the Aldine Greek Horae.

Between 1516 and 1529 Th. Martens (or rather Rescius for him) brought out no less than eight editions of single dialogues of Lucian in Greek, three Homers, three speeches by Demosthenes, two Aesops, two Xenophons, two Isocrates, Plutarch, Cebes, Euripides, the *Plutus* of Aristophanes, the *Cratylus* of Plato, Theocritus, Libanius. All little Greek quartos of no great cost, which gave to the undergraduates of Louvain—and elsewhere—exactly what they needed for mastering the language with the help of a competent teacher.

When Th. Martens, at a great age, retired from active business in 1529, his Greek press was carried on by Rutger Rescius partly alone and sometimes in partnership with Jo. Sturmius, the Strassburg educationalist. There can hardly have been a more distinguished pair of scholar printers than these two. Erasmus in 1517 recommended Rescius as his first choice for filling the Greek professorship in Busleiden's College.* After much humming and hawing, and after it became clear that no more famous man could be found for the chair at the stipend offered, Rescius was in 1519 appointed the first Greek professor in the Collegium Trilingue, a post he filled with great success till his death in 1545. During the same period he kept up his steady output of Greek text-books from his printing office.*

Thomas Anshelm of Baden, another distinguished scholar-printer, moved on from Pforzheim to the university town of Tübingen* in 1511 and continued at work there till 1516. It was certainly the famous John Reuchlin who encouraged him to come. Anshelm had printed his big Hebrew grammar and other works of his at Pforzheim and possessed a fine set of roman, Greek and Hebrew types. It was important for Reuchlin to have this experienced and skilful printer close at hand.

A first-rate craftsman as a printer, Anshelm devoted himself to the humanist cause, publishing many titles on Latin and Greek grammar, including the Aldine Greek grammar, and even some books on Hebrew. I count thirteen titles by Reuchlin himself among his output. Anshelm was lucky, so to speak, that during his period of activity at Tübingen the feud between the Cologne theologians and Reuchlin, the 'War of the Jewish Books', reached its most violent phase. Pamphlets like Reuchlin's *Augenspiegel* (1511) and his *Defensio contra Calumniatores suos Colonienses* (1513 and 1514) must have found a very big and rapid sale. So did, no doubt, the collection of letters from all the most eminent scholars addressed

PLATE II

The printer Johan Froben by Hans Holbein

to Reuchlin in which they rallied to take his side in the quarrel, the *Epistolae Clarorum Virorum* of March 1514.

Still, it seems that Anshelm found Tübingen an unsatisfactory place to work from, for what reason we know not. After a seemingly successful stay of five years he moved on to Hagenau in Alsace and continued his activities as a printer and bookseller there for several years more. It is not unlikely that the cause of dissatisfaction lay in the disturbed political situation in the Duchy of Württemberg, and that working conditions and perhaps taxation were generally easier in an Imperial Free City like Hagenau. There can be no question though, that Anshelm's standing as a scholar and as a greatly respected counsellor of the Tübingen faculty were not impaired by his removal. When Reuchlin died in 1522, it was on Anshelm's recommendation that the Senate of Tübingen filled the vacant Hebrew professorship with the Cambridge man Robert Wakefield,* paying even his travelling expenses from Louvain.

Our survey of the university towns of Europe where printing was carried on in the first quarter of the sixteenth century has shown us that by no means all presses that catered for the humanists were necessarily doomed to failure. No doubt that printers relying exclusively on patronage could not prosper, and that the commercial, bookselling, factor was all-important for durability and success. Local buyers in a small university town never could suffice for a mass-producing industry, and a domicile remote from the main lines of world traffic proved an insuperable obstacle to the adequate distribution of a thousand or more copies of one book. Printers tended to abandon isolated seats of learning, where they may have enjoyed a monopoly, and to converge on the big trading centres, where competition was great, but where the facilities for reaching many possible markets and book-fairs were easily available.

The printer's own scholarly attainments, and his close collaboration with local scholars as editors and correctors, were of great importance. Brilliant and famous men like Beroaldus and Pius at Bologna, or Budé and Aleander at Paris, could carry a printer to prosperity; saleable copy in constant supply is an essential condition of all publishing. But after all, as in every human enterprise, that undefinable combination of qualities which we call personality remains the determining factor of success or failure. Of all the printers of humanist literature, by far the greatest and most successful (next to the pioneer Aldus Manutius) was John Froben of

Basle. On no account can we omit him from our tale of printers serving the humanist cause; he stands in the forefront. Basle was a university town as well as an Imperial Free City and a most active trading centre on the Rhine. But we hear very little of Froben's relations with the professors of Basle University. He brought in his scholarly helpers like Beatus Rhenanus and ultimately Erasmus himself from outside.

Froben was born in the small Franconian township of Hammelburg about 1460. He began to work at Basle in the printing house of Jo. Amerbach and became a Basle citizen in 1490. In 1491 he first appears as an independent printer, his first book being a one-volume small octavo 'pocket' Bible, in itself a new departure. He took his share in the great editions of St Augustine and other Fathers with Amerbach and Petri, and his work remains distinguished but traditional. Not till 1513 did he definitely turn towards the New Learning with a sure instinct for its coming possibilities. In 1514 he started using Greek type. By 1516 he printed Erasmus' Greek Testament and the first of the nine volumes of Erasmus' edition of St Jerome. There is no need to give a more detailed account of Froben's achievement. By the end of his life (1527) he had seven presses running. Hans Holbein was his artistic assistant and designed his initials and borders. Erasmus lived in his house and remained at hand, not only as a best-selling author, but also as an expert adviser on the quality of the staff of correctors and readers Froben must have employed. It is strange that no bibliographical monograph has been devoted so far to that truly great Renaissance figure.

Aldus, Badius, Thierry Martens and Froben are the men who really accomplished what John Siberch so feebly attempted against impossible odds.

NOTES

Francis Jenkinson. See the Prefaces and Notes by Bradshaw, Gray and Jenkinson to the facsimile reprints of Bullock's *Oratio* (1886), the '*Augustinus*' (1896), the *Hermathena* (1886); also Robert Bowes and G. J. Gray, *John Siberch, Bibliographical Notes* (1906); E. Gordon Duff, *The English Provincial Printers, Stationers and Bookbinders to 1557* (Cambridge, 1912); S. C. Roberts, *A History of the Cambridge University Press, 1521–1921* (Cambridge, 1921).

PAGE I

Jo. Caesarius of Cologne. See P. S. Allen, *Opus Epistolarum* III, p. 262 (Ep. 808). On Jo. Caesarius see Allen's note in *Op. Ep.* II, p. 172 and below p. 35.

one of his bindings. See F. J. H. Jenkinson, 'On a Letter from P. Kaetz to J. Siberch', in *Proceedings of Camb. Antiq. Soc.* VII, p. 186; G. J. Gray, *The Earlier Cambridge Stationers and Bookbinders and the First Cambridge Printer* (Bibl. Soc. 1904), pp. 54–61.

Richard Croke of Eton and King's. J. T. Sheppard, *Richard Croke* (Cambridge, 1919); also Erasmus, Epp. 415, 553. See G. Bauch, 'Die Anfänge des Studiums d. griech. Sprache u. Litt. in Norddeutschland', in *Mitt. d. Ges. f. deutsche Erziehungs- und Schulgeschichte*, VI (1896), pp. 177 ff.

William Grocyn at London. Erasmus, Ep. 227, recommending Croke to John Colet in 1511: 'quondam minister et discipulus Grocini.' See Allen's note there (*Op. Ep.* I, p. 467).

Jerome Aleander at Paris. See Aleander's letter to Erasmus (*Ep.* 256): 'Crocus communis discipulus noster'.

'Encomium Moriae' through the press. See Erasmus' letter to Botzheim (*Op. Ep.* I, p. 19): 'aderam Lutetiae cum per Ricardum Crocum pessimis formulis depravatissime excuderetur.'

godfather of one of his sons. See Leon Dorez, 'Une Lettre de Gilles de Gourmont à Girol. Aleandro', in *Revue des Bibliothèques* (1898), p. 206. See also L. Delaruelle, *Répertoire de la Correspondance de G. Budé* (1907), p. 86, note 4 to a Greek letter from Budé to Croke, Paris, 3 Nov. 1519.

publicum professorem ama. A copy in C.U.L. Of Croke's teaching in Louvain and Cologne we find otherwise no trace, and have to accept his word for it. At Leipzig he stayed nearly four years and had among his pupils there Jo. Camerarius and others.

PAGE 2

held in July 1519. Printed at Paris by Simon de Colines in 1520; an imperfect copy in the British Museum.

came to Cambridge in the same year. I cannot see that the 'divers books' seized by one Thomas Cots, stationer, in September 1520, about which the University of Cambridge intervened with the Lord Mayor, can 'reasonably refer' only to these *Rudimenta*. See H. G. Pollard, 'The Company of Stationers before 1557', in *The Library*, vol. XVIII (1937), p. 25. That very obscure document may refer to any parcel of books that some foreign bookseller was suspected of offering for sale within the City of London, if the alien was for some reason under the University's protection. It may well be that Siberch was that alien.

administration of the University finances. See G. J. Gray, *Cambridge Stationers*, pp. 55–60, and, correcting himself, Gray's communication to E. Gordon Duff, *The English Provincial Printers, Stationers and Bookbinders to 1557* (Cambridge, 1912), pp. 74–5.

incorporated M.A. On Wakefield see the note by P. S. Allen in *Op. Ep.* v, p. 123 and with a little more detail, H. de Vocht, *History of the Collegium Trilingue*, I (1951), pp. 379–86. Whatever his solid attainments as a linguist (he taught Hebrew, Arabic and Syriac) may have been, his career was a spectacular one. He taught at Louvain in 1519, and was called to Tübingen as Reuchlin's successor in 1522. He was appointed Hebrew professor at Cambridge in 1523 and there delivered an *Oratio de Laudibus trium linguarum*, printed by Wynkyn de Worde in 1524. From 1532 he taught at Oxford, where he was made a canon of Christ Church (then the King's new College). He died in 1537.

two of his ten books. On Bullock see C. H. and T. Cooper, *Athenae Cantabrigienses*, I (1858), pp. 33–4, 527; Allen, *Op. Ep.* I, 465.

PAGE 5

Froben at Basle. 'The central portion of this letter bears a general resemblance to the "Apologia" prefixed to the Novum Instrumentum, 1516, some passages being almost verbally embodied. It was perhaps elaborated for publication as a further defence of that volume' (Allen, *Op. Ep.* II, p. 221).

PAGE 6

in August 1522. Allen, *Op. Ep.* v, no. 1284.

whatever it is made of. See also Erasmus' autobiographical letter to John Botzheim, Allen, *Op. Ep.* I, p. 9: Annotaram quaedam Anglo cuidam De Ratione conscribendarum epistolarum, sed non in hoc ut aederentur. Eo defuncto, quum viderem opus, ut erat mutilum et mendosum, aeditum in Anglia, coactus sum paucos dies in eiusmodi nugis perdere, quas plane cupiebam abolitas, si qua fieri potuisset.

Robert Fisher. See full biographical note in H. de Vocht, *Jerome de Busleyden* (1950), p. 38. Studied at Padua. J. U. D. 1502. In 1503 styled 'the Kyngs solicitor at Rome'. Canon of St George's, Windsor, 1509. In 1511 his Windsor canonry was given to Wolsey, so that he was presumably dead by then.

PAGE 7

must remain an open question. See Allen, *Op. Ep.* I, no. 241, to Roger Wentford. That others before Siberch had access to the MS. and quoted from it we learn from Erasmus, Ep. 341, lines 10–12.

a man from the Netherlands. Holonius, who was from Liége, Belgium.

PAGE 9

to Robert Aldrich. Later Provost of Eton, 1536 and Bishop of Carlisle, 1537; see the note on him prefixed to this letter (Ep. 1656) by Allen, *Op. Ep.* VI, p. 243.

PAGE 10

entirely open. Occasionally but by no means frequently we meet with an imperial privilege professing to afford protection against reprints within the whole extent of the Holy Roman Empire. Such patents must in practice have been almost completely abortive. The imperial jurisdiction was much too expensive, too dilatory and too clumsy to be set in motion in such a comparatively small matter. At least I know of no record of a single 'leading case' when such a privilege was effectively invoked against a transgressor. K. Schottenloher has given a list of imperial privileges in early books in the *Gutenberg Jahrbuch*, VIII (1933), pp. 89–110.

There are also a few papal privileges professing to extend protection over the whole of Christendom through the ecclesiastical courts, and there is at least one famous instance of such a patent being enforced. The first complete edition of Tacitus' *Annals* (Rome, 1515), carries such a privilege. The book was reprinted at Milan, i.e. outside the territorial jurisdiction of the Pope, in 1517. The Milanese authorities in accordance with the privilege, descended upon the printer Alex. Minutianus; he was heavily fined and the remaining copies of his reprint were confiscated. It is true that this was a book in which Pope Leo X took a great personal interest.

PAGE 11

P. S. Allen. In *Transactions of the Bibliographical Society*, XIII (1916), pp. 297–322; reprinted in Allen's *Erasmus* (Oxford, 1934), pp. 109–37.

De Octo Orationis Partium Constructione. Bowes and Gray, *John Siberch* (1906), p. 25, no. 9.

the work of Lily or of Erasmus. See Allen, *Op. Ep.* i, p. 9: Ad (J. Coleti) preces castigavi libellum Lilii, quem suo ludo praefecerat, de Syntaxi, sed mutatis tam multis ut nec Lilius vellet opus agnoscere nec ego possem.

at London in 1513. S.T.C. 10497 under Erasmus; for later English impressions see S.T.C. 15602–5 under Lily.

PAGE 12

Lily's share in the book. See Allen, *Op. Ep.* ii, no. 341.

Aristotle himself. His translations of Aristotle never appeared in print, and seem to be lost; nor do we have his translations of *Simplicius on the 'Physics'* or of *Alexander Aphrodisiensis on the 'Meteora'*, which he had promised to the printer Aldus in 1499; see Aldus' preface to Linacre's *Proclus on the Sphere.*

PAGE 14

near the end of the century. On Linacre see the excellent introduction of Dr J. F. Payne to the facsimile edition of the Cambridge Galen (Cambridge, 1881). Also Sir William Osler, *Thomas Linacre* (Cambridge, 1908), and Sandys, *History of Classical Scholarship*, ii (Cambridge, 1908), pp. 225–8.

a different context. See E. P. Goldschmidt, *Medieval Texts and their First Appearance in Print* (1943), pp. 45–6.

PAGE 15

a universal Deluge in 1524. Lynn Thorndike, *History of Magic and Experimental Science*, v (1941), pp. 178–233, gives a whole chapter (xi) to the Conjunction of 1524 and cites G. Hellmann's paper in *Beiträge zur Geschichte der Meteorologie* (1914) (Veröffentlichungen des Kgl. Preussischen Meteorologischen Instituts, Berlin) where 133 titles by 56 authors are bibliographically described, the earliest being, it would seem, one of 1519 and that opposing the already widespread anxiety.

promised to refund them to you. See Allen, *Op. Ep.* ii, no. 328, lines 38 and 55. Also in another letter from Rhenanus, *Op. Ep.* ii, no. 330: Salvus sit Dinckelius. Allen in his note surmises this Duncellus might be Froben's son Jerome. Since he calls himself Joannes here that cannot stand. But he must have been a relative of Froben who would not otherwise undertake to pay for clothes of Erasmus' servant.

PAGE 16

by Nicholas Wilson. Nicholas Wilson in 1538 became Master of Michaelhouse and died in 1548. See Cooper, i, p. 94.

the pseudo-philosophers. 'Palliatorum turba qui personatos simulantes philosophos [the "palliatorum", I suspect, alludes to the gowns of the Masters and Doctors in Divinity] estimantes nullam disciplinam esse extra eorum caninam loquentiam.' To this passage we find the marginal gloss, on F. 3: 'Nullos hic theologos taxat, nisi hos qui spreta eloquentia nec veteres theologos intelligant.'

the quibbling lawyers. '...quod ad publicam utilitatem religionemve pertinet, id vulgatissimo pedestrique sermone scribi oportere.'

PAGE 17

dedicated to Richard Pace. See Jervis Wegg, *Richard Pace, a Tudor Diplomatist* (London, 1932), a book, as the title implies, mainly devoted to Pace's activities as a statesman, and somewhat perfunctory on his writings and scholarly interests.

a theme recalled in the 'Hermathena'. 'Aderat forte unus ex his, quos nos generosos vocamus et qui semper cornu aliquod a tergo pendens gestant, ac si etiam inter prandendum venarentur.' This 'generosus' is made to say, '...omnes docti sunt mendici, etiam Erasmus....'

Bradshaw wrote in 1886. In his Bibliographical Introduction to the facsimile edition of Bullock's *Oratio* (Cambridge, 1886), p. 21.

PAGE 18

before 1585. I am aware of F. Madan's claim for the existence of two presses at Oxford in 1517–18, those of John Scolar and of Charles Kyrfoth, but on typographical grounds I venture to reject it. The few small quartos bearing the names and Oxford addresses of these two men are indubitably printed by Wynkyn de Worde in London. All the three types found in these books, as well as the woodcuts, are in Wynkyn de Worde's possession both before and after their publication. According to the rules we generally observe in making press attributions, it appears much more plausible to assume that these books were printed by de Worde on commission and for sale by Scolar or Kyrfoth from their Oxford premises, rather than a wandering to and fro of the printing equipment for such an insignificant purpose.

PAGE 20

in the hands of Antwerp printers. See McKerrow and Ferguson, Title-page borders no. 10.

PAGE 21

another seventy years. According to Herbert, *Typogr. Antiq.* III, Pref., the first Greek book printed in England was *Jo. Chrysostomus Homiliae duae*, ed. John Cheke, London, Reyner Wolfe, 1543 (*S. T. C.* 14634). This is however a very isolated forerunner, and the first printer to issue Greek classics regularly is G. Bishop from 1590 onwards.

PAGE 23

impact on European letters. See Appendix B, 'Renaissance Translations from the Greek', pp. 72 ff. below.

Archbishop Warham in 1506. On the genesis of this translation and the circumstances of the dedication see Erasmus' letter to Botzheim, Allen, *Op. Ep.* I, pp. 4–5.

what Greek they knew. Sandys, *History of Classical Scholarship*, II, pp. 83–4; Sir Richard Jebb in *Cambridge Modern History*, I, p. 555.

PAGE 24

the Medicean and the Vatican Libraries. C. Cipolla, *L'Azione Letteraria di Niccolo V nel Rinascimento* (Frosinone, 1900).

PAGE 26

Francesco Griffolini of Arezzo. Gir. Mancini, *Francesco Griffolini cognominato Francesco Aretino* (Firenze, 1890), G. Mercati, *Scritti d'Isidoro il Cardinale Rutheno* (*Studi e Testi*, 46) (Rome, 1926), Appendice V, pp. 128–32, 'Francesco Aretino in Oriente'.

Griffolini's 'Phalaris' in 1485. Gordon Duff, *Fifteenth-Century English Books*, no. 348.

PAGE 27

ut mos est apud Anglos. See his letter to Botzheim in Allen, *Op. Ep.* I, p. 8, lines 7–8; also H. W. Garrod, 'Erasmus and his English Patrons', in *The Library*, fifth series, vol. IV (1949), pp. 1–13.

PAGE 28

earliest to be translated. The *Charon* and the *Timon* are turned into Latin before 1403. See E. P. Goldschmidt, 'The First Edition of Lucian of Samosata', in *Journal of the Warburg and Courtauld Institutes*, XIV (1951), pp. 7–20.

the best brains of Europe. On Lucian in the Renaissance see Rich. Förster in *Archiv für Literaturgeschichte*, XIV (1886), pp. 337–63, and again with special reference to the works of art based on the *Calumnia* in the *Jahrbuch d. K. preussischen Kunstsammlungen*, VIII (1887), and XV (1894). Further: C. R. Thompson, *The Translations of Lucian by Erasmus and St Thomas More* (Ithaca N.Y., 1940), and the same author's more extensive Princeton dissertation, *Lucian and Lucianism in the English Renaissance* (1937), of which a photostat copy is to be found at the Warburg Institute, London.

PAGE 29

in every university of Christendom. R. Weiss, 'England and the Decree of the Council of Vienne', in *Mélanges Renaudet* (1952) = *Bibl. d'Humanisme et Renaissance*, XIV, pp. 1–9.

PAGE 30

the Collège de France by 1530. Abel Lefranc, *Histoire du Collège de France* (1893), p. 43.

PAGE 31

William Selling, who died in 1495. On the early English Graecists see R. Weiss, *Humanism in England during the Fifteenth Century* (Oxford, 1941). None of them is of great importance, but it would be difficult if not impossible to find a comparable number of scholars able to translate from the Greek in fifteenth-century France or Germany.

their connection with Erasmus and More. P. S. Allen, *Erasmus. Lectures and Wayfaring Sketches* (Oxford, 1934), p. 150.

caused so little friction. Erasmus' letter to P. Mosellanus 1519, Allen, *Op. Ep.* III, no. 948, lines 183 ff.

PAGE 32

letter cited above. In the last note to p. 31.

a preponderant importance. Erasmus took his D.D. at Turin on 4 September 1506, almost at his first stop on Italian soil and during a stay of a very few days only. It must have been a very informal formality.

PAGE 34

studied at Louvain in 1479. See H. de Vocht, *Hist. of...Collegium Trilingue* (1951), pp. 174–5. The fact, if it is a fact, that Fox completed his studies at Louvain is not known to his English biographers. Practically nothing is known about him before he emerges as bishop of Exeter in 1487 and Lord Privy Seal. However, the entry in the Louvain matriculation list cited by de Vocht: 'Mgr Ricardus Fox lincolnens. dyoc. in decretis. 5 June 1479', fits in so well with his biographical data that it would be surprising if it were no more than a coincidence and the two were not identical.

PAGE 36

learned their Greek from him. See Allen's note in *Op. Ep.* II, 172. See also above, p. 1, for his acquaintance with Siberch.

Peter Tomai of Ravenna, in 1506–8. The Petrus Ravennas episode is notable because the offended Italian, when expelled from Cologne, printed a farewell letter in the most atrocious dog Latin, as used by his opponents, which undoubtedly became the inspiration and the model for the *Epistolae Obscurorum Virorum.* See de Vocht, *Trilingue,* pp. 299 and 419, and the sources cited there.

the Pope himself. On the 'Judenbücher-streit' see Boecking, *Hutteni Operum Supplementum,* 1864–9; L. Geiger, *Jo. Reuchlin* (1871); *Epistolae Obscurorum Virorum,* ed. F. G. Stokes (London, 1909).

at Hagenau in Alsace. See A. Bömer, 'Die Fünf Frühdrucke der Epistolae Obscurorum Virorum', in *Beiträge zum Bibliotheks- und Buchwesen Paul Schwenke gewidmet* (Berlin, 1913), pp. 17–29.

PAGE 37

or you would not have done it. See Stokes, *E.O.V.*, pp. 20 and 301–2. I use Stokes' valiant attempt at a translation. In reality these letters are quite untranslatable because half their fun lies in their atrocious distortion of Latin.

he would also come to Leipzig. See Stokes, *E.O.V.*, pp. 253 and 508; for other references to Croke in *E.O.V.* see pp. 91 and 149. For Hutten's letter to Croke from Bologna, 22 August 1516, see p. lxv of Stokes' Introduction.

lectured there as early as 1467. His public announcement of his lectures on Terence in 1470 is found in a MS. written by Hieronymus Münzer, now in C.U.L. (Add.6676, fo. 120^b).

PAGE 39

in full swing at Leipzig. See A. Renaudet, *Préréforme et Humanisme à Paris (1494–1517)*, Preface, pp. v–vi: '...l'histoire des idées, celle de l'humanisme, celle même de faits qui, à première vue, semblent étrangers à l'histoire religieuse,—comme l'introduction des études grecques en France—, deviennent infiniment plus intelligibles, et nous apparaissent plus aisément sous leur veritable jour, si l'on n'oublie jamais que la question de la réforme du clergé dans son chef et dans ses membres, des rapports de l'Eglise de France avec l'Eglise de Rome, du concile avec le pape, dominent alors toutes les intelligences, et que, dans les collèges où travaillent Lefèvre, ses disciples, ou les lecteurs d'Erasme, on suit passionément la restauration de la discipline cléricale et de l'idéal chrétien.'

PAGE 41

ornaments from Cologne. See *Cambridge Bibl. Soc. Trans.* I, pp. 42–5.

the 'Sertorius variety'. See Proctor, II, p. 193.

patron of printing. On Marschalk and his publishing activities at Erfurt, Wittenberg and Rostock see G. Bauch, 'Wolfgang Schenk und Nicolaus Marschalk', in *Centralblatt f. Bibliothekswesen*, XII (1895), pp. 353 ff. Also G. Bauch, *Erfurt im Zeitalter des Frühhumanismus* (Breslau, 1904), pp. 189–220. A very substantial account of the man and his writings is found in J. A. Fabricius, *Bibliotheca med. & inf. Lat.* (1858), VI, pp. 559–64 s.v. '*Thurius*' (by C. Schöttgen).

the university of Erfurt. Erfurt was a university under the archbishop of Mayence, of which the origins (organised colleges) go back to the twelfth century. It was properly 'founded' as a *studium generale* by a privilege of the Avignon Pope Clement VII in 1379 and again by the Roman Pope Urban VI in 1389.

At the period with which we are concerned Martin Luther was an undergraduate there (see Rashdall, *Medieval Universities* (1936), II, pp. 245–50).

in Northern Germany at any rate. See Proctor, *Printing of Greek in the Fifteenth Century* (1900), p. 139, who reproduces the type from a 'Kanzleibüchlein' of 1500, overlooking the 1499 Psellus, of which only three copies are known. See also G. Bauch, 'Die Anfänge des Studiums der griechischen Sprache in Norddeutschland', in *Mitt. d. Ges. f. deutsche Erziehungs- u. Schulgeschichte*, VI, pp. 50–1.

PAGE 42

the identity of the type. Proctor, II, p. 158: 'Though the name of Sertorius is not found at Wittenberg, the identity of the type is certain, and its transfer corresponds with the removal of Marschalk to Wittenberg from Erfurt.'

signed by him in 1504. A Cantalycius on the Judgment of Paris and on Pyramus and Thisbe, Panzer, IX, 66, 3. On Trebelius as the first printer at Wittenberg see G. Bauch, *Erfurt im Zeitalter des Frühhumanismus*, pp. 155–6 and 182–5. Also, quite recently, Jos. Benzing, 'Hermann Trebelius, Dichter und Drucker zu Wittenberg und Eisenach', in *Das Antiquariat* IX (Wien, 1953), pp. 203–4. Proctor 11233 (Εἰσαγωγὴ πρὸς τῶν γραμμάτων Ἑλλήνων) should be transferred from Erfurt to Trebelius' press at Wittenberg.

PAGE 43

sed Romanis literis excussit. See G. Bauch, 'Drucke von Frankfurt a.O.' in *Centralblatt f. Bibliothekswesen*, XV (1898), pp. 241–60. In 1514 Johannes Jamer de Hanau calls himself 'tunc temporis Francophordiani studii calcographus'. The roman type used by the Frankfurt a.O. printers is not of the 'Sertorius variety' but a more ordinary roman fount resembling Basle types.

PAGE 44

private printing establishment. On Marschalk's Rostock press see, besides G. Bauch's paper cited above p. 42, the earlier articles by Lisch and Wiechmann-Kadow cited by Proctor, II, p. 115.

PAGE 45

Giovanni Ricuzzi of Camerino. On the early Vienna humanists see G. Bauch, *Die Reception des Humanismus in Wien* (1903) and K. Grossmann, 'Die Frühzeit des Humanismus in Wien bis zu Celtis' Berufung' in *Jahrbuch f. Landeskunde v. Niederösterreich*, XXII (1929), pp. 150–325. On the period after 1500 we are much less well informed, for vol. II of J. Aschbach's *Gesch. d. Wiener Universität* (1877), which professes to deal with it, is a sadly confused and unreliable book; but Michael Denis' *Wiens Buchdruckergeschichte bis 1560* is more than adequate.

PAGE 47

for many details. Renaudet's book, with the bibliographies brought up to date, has just been reprinted in 1953. A. Tilley's *Dawn of the French Renaissance* (Cambridge, 1918), has excellent chapters on the subject that concerns us, besides placing it within the wider survey of French art and culture, both in Paris and in the provinces; but unfortunately Tilley's book, in despite of the date on the title, was completely printed by 1915 and, owing to the war, he does not even seem to have seen Renaudet's work before his own was published.

desire for Greek studies (1501). See Allen, *Op. Ep.* I, p. 7: 'Graece balbutiebat sed talis ut neque potuisset docere si voluisset, neque voluisset si potuisset,' and Allen's note there. Also *Ep.* 138, 41 and *Ep.* 149, 65–8.

PAGE 48

Jodocus Badius van Assche of Ghent. On Badius as a scholar see Tilley, *Dawn of the French Renaissance*, pp. 214 ff. On his achievement as a printer we have the masterly study by Ph. Renouard, *Bibliographie des Impressions de Josse Badius Ascensius, Imprimeur et Humaniste, 1462–1535* (Paris, 1908), 3 vols.

his Greek Testament of 1516. Erasmus' dedication to Christopher Fisher sums up his attitude to Biblical text studies concisely; and he adhered to it for the rest of his life. If it was permissible for Nicolaus de Lyra to correct the Old Testament according to the Hebrew original, why should it be reprehensible to correct the New Testament according to the Greek? Grammar, i.e. philological studies, was subsidiary, but necessary to theology. Even here we get a citation of the Decree of Vienne (1311) enjoining Greek studies in all universities. See Allen, *Op. Ep.* I, pp. 406–12 (*Ep.* 182).

PAGE 49

Paulus Diaconus (1514). See E. P. Goldschmidt, *Medieval Texts* (1943), pp. 72–5.

edition of the 'Adagia' in 1500. It contains only 823 proverbs; the second printed by Badius in 1507 has only twenty more, but the Aldine edition of 1508 has as many as 3260 and the number continues to grow in subsequent editions.

Gilles de Gourmont. See Ph. Renouard, *Imprimeurs Parisiens* (1898), p. 158. W. P. Greswell, *A View of the Early Parisian Greek Press* (1833), 2 vols, is no longer of much use, except that it places Gourmont's press in perspective with the much greater achievements of the Estienne's, Wechel's, etc., soon to follow. The best account will be found in H. A. Omont, 'Essai sur les Débuts de la Typographie grecque à Paris', in *Mémoires de la Société de l'Histoire de Paris*, XVIII (1892), pp. 1–72; Proctor, *Printing of Greek* (1900), p. 142. On Tissard's translation of Euripides, see P. de Nolhac's 'Le premier travail français sur Euripide; la traduction de Francois Tissard', in *Mélanges Weil* (Paris, 1898).

PAGE 50

Jerome Aleander. See Allen's Note in *Op. Ep.* I, p. 502; his *Life* by J. Paquier (1900) and his *Lettres Familières*, ed. J. Paquier (1909). H. A. Omont published his Diaries in *Notices et Extraits des MSS.* xxxv (1896). L. Delaruelle, 'Un Recueil d'Adversaria autographes de Girolamo Aleandro', in *Mélanges...de l'Ecole française de Rome*, xx (1900).

Before he left Aleander was elected Rector of Paris University in 1512. It may be worth noting that one of Aleander's most successful Paris courses was on Ausonius, and that his pupil Croke lectured on Ausonius and edited him at Leipzig in 1515; no doubt using the notes he had made at Paris. There exists considerable literature on Aleander as Papal Legate in Germany and on his preparatory endeavours for the Council of Trent, but this lies outside our time-limit.

PAGE 51

abandoned his Greek courses in January 1509. Aleander writes to Aldus in Venice that he has foiled Tissard's plans and that he will not lecture any more (Tandem li ho ropto il disegno et credo che collui piu non leza). Cited by Omont, 'Débuts d. l. Typogr. grecque'.

press of Caen. On Caen see A. Tilley, *Studies in the French Renaissance* (1922), pp. 1–11, and L. Delisle, *Catalogue des Livres imprimés ou publiés à Caen avant le milieu du XVIe siècle, suivi de recherches sur les imprimeurs et les libraires de la même ville* (Caen, 1903–4), 2 vols.

of Toulouse. On Toulouse see T. Desbarreaux-Bernard, 'L'imprimerie à Toulouse au XVIme siècle', in *Mémoires de l'Académie des Sciences...de Toulouse, VIII série*, vol. I (1879), pp. 216–38.

Poitiers. On Poitiers see A. Claudin, *Origines et Débuts de l'Imprimerie à Poitiers* (Paris, 1897), and A. Claudin, *Bibliographie par ordre chronologique des premiers livres imprimés à Poitiers 1497–1515* (Paris, 1897).

PAGE 52

Robert de Keysere. Robert de Keysere of Gent was an interesting character rather than an important printer. He starts his press at Gent in 1510 with a little Erasmus item, soon migrates to Paris where he brings out five or six more titles, including Aleander's *Tabulae*, and returns to Gent by 1513, where another six books issue from his press. In Paris in 1511 he seems to have been the head of the Collège de Tournai and he continues to teach at Gent, encouraged by Erasmus' approving letters. In 1523 he even starts a project for a university of his own at Tournai. See on him de Vocht, *Collegium Trilingue* (1951), pp. 279–81 and the references cited there. For his production as a printer, M. E. Kronenberg in *Handelingen van het Tweede Congres voor Boek- en Bibliotheekwezen* (Gent, 1932), pp. 175–200, and further in *Het Boek*, xxiv (1936), pp. 41–55.

died at Milan in 1521. On J. P. d'Angleberme see Allen, *Op. Ep.* I, pp. 329–30 and the literature cited there. Add the references given in the 'Journal autobiographique de Jerome Aleandre', publ. by H. A. Omont in *Notices et Extraits des MSS.* xxxv (1896), p. 18.

PAGE 53

New Learning in Europe. Rashdall, *Medieval Universities* (1936), II, pp. 266–7.

Thierry Martens of Alost. A. F. van Iseghem, *Biographie de Thierry Martens d'Alost* (Malines, Alost, 1852; Suppl. 1866). For his correct dates of birth and death, 1446/7–1534, see C. Reedijk, 'Dirk Martens van Alst en Servaes van Sassen', in *Het Boek*, xxxi (1952), pp. 52–7.

Rutger Rescius. On Rescius see Allen's note in *Op. Ep.* II, p. 497; and de Vocht, *Collegium Trilingue*, esp. pp. 277–9 and 294.

PAGE 54

Busleiden's College. Allen, *Op. Ep.* no. 691, 14–17; 'Est hic Rutgerus, iuvenis optimus et eruditior quam prae se ferat, sed malim rem, ut dixi, per celebres et eximios institui.'

from his printing office. See Nijhoff-Kronenberg, *Nederlandsche Bibliographie*, I (1923), pp. 856–8; II (1940), pp. 1002–4.

the university town of Tübingen. K. Steiff, *Der erste Buchdruck in Tübingen, 1498–1534* (Tübingen, 1881).

PAGE 55

Robert Wakefield. On Wakefield see above p. 2 and note 58. On Anshelm as his sponsor, de Vocht, *Coll. Trilingue*, p. 382.

APPENDIX A

LIST OF BULLOCK'S BOOKS

Henry Bullock died in 1526. A list of his books taken over by Queens' College after his death is preserved in the College archives. Cooper's *Ath. Cantab.* I, p. 34 gives but an obscure hint of its existence ('His library, a catalogue of which is extant, was purchased by Queens' College'). Thanks to the kind and efficient help of the Rev. H. St J. Hart, Librarian of that college, I have succeeded in tracing this vague statement to its source and can furnish a transcription of this catalogue:

Queens' College MSS. of the Rev. W. G. Searle; Notebook 4, p. 88: Extracts from a volume containing Compositions for Fellowships, Forinseca Recepta 1529–1558, Computus Finalis 1503–1529, Fol. 77 b:

Computus Simonis Heynes de omnibus libris per eundem venditis et appreciatis qui olim erant D. Bullock:

1	*Opera hieronimi*	xxxs.
2	*Annotationes Erasmi*	vis. viiid.
3	*Opera Ambrosii in 3*	vs. viiid.
4	*Historia Germanorum*	iis. viiid.
5	*Rhetorica Tullii* (m. Carleton)	xvid.
6	*Roffensis contra Lutherum*	iis. ivd.
7	*Dioscorides* (m. Heynes)	xiid.
8	*Julius Pollux* (m. Wilkes)	vs.
9	*Biblia Graeca*	xs. iiid.
10	*Aristoteles de Animalibus, Problemata Theophrastus de Plantis*	xxs.
11	*Adagia magna Erasmi*	xiis. iiid.
12	*Fabule Esopi grece*	iis. iiid.
13	*Homerus et Macrobius*	iiis.
14	*Corpus Juris Civilis*	viiis.
15	*hiliados Homeri grece*	iis.
16	*Methodus medendi Galeni*	xvid.
17	*Odissea Homeri latine*	xiid.
18	*Suetonius*	iis.
19	*Pyndarus poeta graece*	xiid.

20	*Grammatica Theodori Gaze*	xvi d.
21	*Dioscorides graece*	ii s. iiii d.
22	*Tragedie Euripidis grece*	xvi d.
23	*Odissea Homeri grece*	xvi d.
24	*Opera Zenophonis Philosophi grece*	ii s. iiii d.

All these be cheyned in the College library except III before rehearsed.

The 'Three before rehearsed' are presumably nos. 5, 7 and 8 acquired by Gerard Carleton, Fellow of Queens', died as dean of Peterborough 1549 (Cooper, *Ath. Cantab.* I, p. 95); Simon Heynes, President of Queens', d. 1552 (Cooper, I, p. 111); and Richard Wilkes, Fellow of Queens', later Master of Christ's, d. 1556 (Cooper, I, p. 162).

BIBLIOGRAPHICAL NOTES

1 Hieronymus, *Opera*, ed. Erasmus, Basle, Froben 1516 or 1520. 5 vols. fol.

2 *Annotationes Erasmi* = presumably the Annotationes in Novum Testamentum which form a part of the 1519 and 1522 Basle editions of the Greek N.T.

3 Ambrosius, *Opera*. Probably the Basle, Adam Petri 1516 edition or an earlier Basle edition. Erasmus' Ambrosius did not appear till 1527.

4 *Historia Germanorum*. This cannot be the *Rerum Germanicarum libri III* of Beatus Rhenanus, first published in 1531, or Lambert of Hersfeld (1077), *De Rebus gestis Germanorum* (Tübingen, 1525). It is most probably F. Irenicus, *Germaniae Exegeseos volumina XII* (Hagenau, Anshelm, 1518).

5 *Rhetorica Tullii*. There are too many editions of Cicero's *Rhetorica* to permit a guess.

6 *Roffensis contra Lutherum* = St John Fisher, *Assertionis Lutheranae confutatio*. Basle, 1523, or Antwerp, 1523 or Cologne, 1525.

7 *Dioscorides*. See below, no. 21.

8 Julius Pollux, *Vocabularium* (Venice, Aldus, 1502).

9 *Biblia Graeca* = Sacrae Scripturae veteris novaeque omnia (Venice, Aldus, 1518). The O.T. text is that of the Septuagint, the N.T. Erasmus' text of 1516.

10 Aristoteles = Vols III and IV of Aldus' editio princeps of Aristotle (Venice, 1497).

11 *Adagia magna Erasmi*. Probably Venice, Aldus, 1508, or a subsequent edition of which there were many before 1526.

12 *Fabule Esopi graece* (Venice, Aldus, 1505); or Basle, Froben, 1518, 1521, 1524.

13 *Homerus et Macrobius*. Not identifiable.

14 *Corpus Juris Civilis.* Not identifiable.

15 *Homeri Ilias gr.* Probably an Aldine edition 1504 or 1517.

16 Galenus, *Methodus Medendi.* This is Linacre's translation (Paris, D. Maheu, 1519).

17 *Odissea Homeri latine.* May be the Latin prose version by Jo. Tortellius printed at Strassburg by Jo. Schott in 1510 or another version published by Jac. Mazochius at Rome in September 1510.

18 *Suetonius.* Not identifiable.

19 *Pyndarus poeta graece.* Either Venice, Aldus, 1513 or Rome, Zach. Callierges, 1515.

20 Gaza = Th. Gaza (Venice, Aldus, 1495). This copy is still extant in Cambridge University Library (Inc. 2166) in its original binding with Bullock's name 'MAGISTER BULLOKE' written large on the front cover. It later belonged to Sir Thomas Smith and came to ULC after 1658. I owe this information to Mr J. C. T. Oates. See Frontispiece.

21 *Dioscorides graece.* The Greek Dioscorides published by Aldus at Venice, 1499, and again 1518. No. 7, another Dioscorides, not stated to be Greek and estimated at a quarter of this Aldine folio, is presumably a Latin version, perhaps that of Lyons, G. de Villiers, 1512.

22 Euripides. Almost certainly the Aldine edition (Venice, 1503).

23 *Odissea Homeri grece.* Probably the other volume of the Aldine edition of Homer 1504 or 1517; see no. 15.

24 Xenophon. The Aldine edition was only published in April 1525 and may only just have reached Bullock before he died. However this could be the editio princeps (Florence, Giunta, 1516).

APPENDIX B

RENAISSANCE TRANSLATIONS FROM THE GREEK

The prevailing lack of interest in these translations is not of recent date. Neither T. F. Dibdin in his *Introduction to the Classics* (1827), nor B. Botfield in his Prefaces to the Editiones Principes (1861) include them in their investigations, although the latter enumerates some of them briefly in his Preface. J. E. Sandys in his *History of Classical Scholarship*, vol. II (1908) has little to say about them. A few years ago, however, a group of American scholars initiated a collaborative enterprise to establish a list of all medieval and Renaissance translations from the Greek of which we hope to see the results some day.

What I have tried to give in the following brief tabulation is by no means a 'complete' survey of the existing translations. My list confines itself to printed editions and ignores known MSS. The choice of authors included or omitted is quite arbitrary. Short pieces found only in composite volumes are on the whole left out for brevity's sake, but some are listed because they seemed interesting to me. Aristotle, Hippocrates and Galen are not dealt with for no better reason than that their medieval and their Renaissance translations seem inextricably mixed up, and each of them demands a special study for which I am not qualified.

My main purpose in making this list was to give substance to my assertion on p. 23 that these 'printed Latin editions precede by a long time the appearance of the Greek originals'. By giving a fair number of examples I hope to have proved my point. To go beyond that, for example to prove their wide diffusion by listing all the known early editions, would have swelled this Appendix beyond the limits of the permissible.

NOTE. The material in this Appendix is not entered in the Index.

AUTHOR AND TITLE	FIRST GREEK PRINTING	LATIN TRANSLATIONS
AELIANUS *Tactica*	1552, Venice (A. & J. Spinelli)	1487, Rome (E. Silber) *Trs.* THEODORUS GAZA by 1455, *De Instruendis Aciebus* [GW 310]
AESCHINES *In Ctesiphontem*	1513, Venice (Aldus, in *Rhetores Gr.*)	1485, Venice (A. Torresanus & B. de Blavis) *Trs.* OMNIBONUS LEONICENUS (d. 1493) in Cicero, *De Oratore*, etc. [GW 6750]
AESOP *Fabulae*	c. 1480, Milan (Bonus Accursius) [GW 313]	c. 1480, Milan (first printed together with Greek) *Trs.* RINUCCIO OF AREZZO (c. 1440) [GW 313] c. 1472, Utrecht? (Printer of *Speculum*) *Trs.* LORENZO VALLA (c. 1440) [GW 315] c. 1470/1, Venice (Valdarfer) *Trs.* OMNIBONUS LEONICENUS (d. 1493) [GW 333] 1488, Parma (A. Ugoletus) *Trs.* FRANCISCUS MARIA GRAPALDUS (d. 1516) [GW 344a]
AGATHIAS *De Bello Gothorum*, etc.	1660, Paris (in *Agathiae De Rebus Gestis Justiniani (Script. Rer. Byz.)*)*	1516, Rome (Jac. Mazochius) *Trs.* CHR. PERSONA (d. 1486)
ALCINOUS *Introd. ad Dogmata Platonis*	1521, Venice (Aldus, with Apuleius)	1469, Rome (Sweinheym & Pannartz) (with Apuleius) *Trs.* PIETRO BALBI, bp. of Tropea (c. 1460) First separate ed. 1472, Nürnberg (Ant. Koberger) [GW 806]
ALEXANDER APHRODISIENSIS *De Anima*	1534, Venice (Aldus, with Themistius)	1495, Brescia (B. Misinta) *Trs.* HIERON. DONATUS [GW 859]
Problemata	1497, Venice (Aldus, with Aristoteles), vol. IV	1488, Venice (A. de Strata) *Trs.* GEORGIUS VALLA (d. 1499) [GW 860]
APPIANUS *Historia Romana*	1551, Paris (C. Stephanus)	1472, Venice (Vind. de Spira) (second part only) [GW 2293] 1477, Venice (Ratdolt, Maler and Löslein) (both parts) [G 2290] *Trs.* PIER CANDIDO DECEMBRIO (d. 1477)
ARISTEAS *De LXXII interpretibus*	1561, Basle (Oporinus)	1471, Rome (Sweinheym & Pannartz) (first in Biblia lat.) [GW 4210] 1474, Naples (Arn. de Bruxella) (first separate) [GW 2331] or (Naples, S. Riessinger, s.a.) [GW 2330] *Trs.* MAT. PALMERIUS (d. 1478)

* I doubt if the Paris 1660 ed. is really the first Greek. Its editor and commentator is Bonaventura Vulcanius, a sixteenth-century Bruges scholar.

AUTHOR AND TITLE	FIRST GREEK PRINTING	LATIN TRANSLATIONS
ARRIANUS *De Expeditione Alexandri*	1535, Venice (Zanetti)	s.a. Venice (B. de Vitalibus) *Trs.* ? 1508, Pesaro (H. Soncino) *Trs.* B. FACIUS
ATHANASIUS *Opera* *Contra Gentiles*	1600–1, Heidelberg (Commelin)	 1519, Paris (J. Petit) *Trs.* AMBR. TRAVERSARI (d. 1439) 1482, Vicenza (L. Achates) *Trs.* OMNIB. LEONICENUS (d. 1493) [GW 2760]
In Vim Psalmorum		*c.* 1500, Augsburg, Froschauer *Trs.* ANG. POLITIANUS (d. 1494) [GW 2761]
De Variis Quaestionibus		1522, Strassburg (Jo. Knoblouch) (fol. 291 ff.) *Trs.* JO. REUCHLIN
BASILIUS *De Legendis Gentilium* *Libris*	*c.* 1496, Florence (L. de Alopa, with Cebes) [GW 6442]	*c.* 1470–1, Venice (Chr. Valdarfer) (and following editions) *Trs.* LEONARDO BRUNI OF AREZZO (d. 1444) [GW 3710–3718]
De Vita Solitaria	1532, Basle (Froben, *Opera*, ed. Erasmus)	1471, Venice (Printer of Basilius) *Trs.* FRANC. PHILELPHUS (d. 1481) [GW 3699]
Hexameron	1532, Basle (Froben, in *Opera*)	1515, Rome (Jac. Mazochius) *Trs.* JO. ARGYROPYLOS (d. 1474) [fol. = Isaac 12122]
'BRUTUS, M.' *Epistolae*	1498, Venice (with Phalaris) [Hain 12871]	*c.* 1474, Rome (Ad. Rot.) [GW 5656] Again with Diogenes, etc. [GW 8396] *Trs.* RINUCCIO OF AREZZO (d. 1458)
CALLIMACHUS *Hymni*	*c.* 1496, Florence (L. de Alopa) [GW 5917]	*c.* 1510, Bologna (B. Hectoris) *Trs.* JAC. CRUCIUS
CEBES *Tabula*	*c.* 1496, Florence (L. de Alopa) [GW 6442]	1497, Bologna (B. Hectoris, with Censorinus) (frequent sixteenth- century reprints) *Trs.* LUD. ODASSI (d. 1510) [GW 6471]
DIO CASSIUS *Historia Romana*	1548, Paris (R. Stephanus)	n.a. 1493, Rome (Printer of Herodianus) *Trs.* BONIF. BEMBO, *Vitae Nervae* *Cocceii Ulpii Trajani* [British Museum, *Early Printed* *Books*, IV, 138]
DIO CHRYSOSTOMUS *De Regno*	1551, Venice (Torresani)	 1470–1, Venice (Chr. Valdarfer) *Trs.* FRANC. PICCOLOMINI by 1469 [GW 8368]
De Troia Non Capta		1492, Cremona (B. Misinta) *Trs.* FRANC. PHILELPHUS (d. 1481) [GW 8370]

AUTHOR AND TITLE	FIRST GREEK PRINTING	LATIN TRANSLATIONS
DIODORUS SICULUS *Historiae*	1539, Basle (Oporinus)	1472, Bologna (Rugerius and Bertochus) *Trs.* POGGIO (d. 1459) [GW 8374]
DIOGENES CYNICUS *Epistolae*	1499, Venice (Aldus, in *Epist.* *Div. Philos.*) [Hain 6659]	*c.* 1475, Nürnberg (F. Creussner) *Trs.* FRANC. GRIFFOLINI OF AREZZO (d. 1460) [GW 8395]
DIOGENES LAERTIUS *Vitae Philosophorum*	1533, Basle (Froben)	1472, Rome (G. Lauer) *Trs.* AMBR. TRAVERSARI (d. 1439)
DIONYSIUS AREOPAGITA *Opera*	1516, Florence (Giunta)	*c.* 1480, Bruges (Colard Mansion) [GW 8408] 1499, Paris (Higman & Hopyl) [GW 8409] *Trs.* AMBR. TRAVERSARI (d. 1439) 1496, Florence (L. de Alopa) *Trs.* MARS. FICINUS (d. 1499) [GW 8410]
DIONYSIUS HALICAR- NASSEUS *Antiquitates* *Romanae*	1546, Paris (Stephanus)	1480, Treviso (B. Celerius de Luere) *Trs.* LAPO BIRAGO [GW 8423]
DIONYSIUS PERIEGETES (=D. Afer) *Orbis* *Descriptio*	1512, Ferrara (Jo. Mazochius)	1477, Venice (Ratdolt, Maler & Löslein)* *Trs.* ANT. BECCARIA [GW 8426]
DIOSCORIDES *De Materia Medica*	1499, Venice (Aldus) [GW 8435]	1478, Colle (Jo. van Medemblick) *Trs.* PETRUS DE ABANO 1250–1316? or earlier? [GW 8436]
EPICTETUS *Enchiridion*	1528, Venice (de Sabio)	1497, Bologna (B. Hectoris, with Censorinus) *Trs.* ANG. POLITIANUS (d. 1494) [GW 6471]
EUCLID *Elementa Geometriae*	1533, Basle (Herwagen)	The first and second Latin editions, Venice, 1482 and Vicenza, 1491 print the twelfth-century transla- tion from the Arabic by ADELARD OF BATH 1505, Venice (Jo. Tacuinus) *Trs.* BART. DEI ZAMBERTI
GREGORIUS NAZIANZENUS *Carmina*	1504, Venice (Aldus, in *Poetae Christiani*)	1531, Basle (Froben & Episcopius) *Trs.* BIL. PIRCKHEIMER, *Orationes* *XXX curante Erasmo*
Orationes Lectissimae *Opera omnia*	1516, Venice (Aldus) 1550, Basle (Hervagius, Greek and Latin)	
HERMES TRISMEGISTUS *Poemander*	1554, Paris (A. Turnebus)	1471, Treviso (G. de Lisa) *Trs.* MARSILIUS FICINUS (d. 1499) [Hain 8456]

* There exists also a late antique translation by 'Fannius' or 'Priscianus', first printed Vienna
c. 1495 [GW 8430]. Both versions are frequently reprinted in the sixteenth century.

AUTHOR AND TITLE	FIRST GREEK PRINTING	LATIN TRANSLATIONS
HERODIANUS *Historia de Imperio post Marcum*	1524, Venice (Aldus)	1493, Rome (Printer of Herodianus) [Hain 8466] 31 Aug. 1493, Bologna (Pl. de Benedictis) Authorised (better) edition *Trs.* ANG. POLIZIANO (d. 1494) [Hain 8467]
HERODOTUS	1502, Venice (Aldus)	1474, Venice (Jac. Rubeus) *Trs.* LOR. VALLA (d. 1457) [Hain 8469]
HESIOD *Opera et Dies*	1481, Milan (B. Accursius, with Theocritus) [Hain 15476]	1471, Rome (Sweinheym & Pannartz, with Silius Ital.) *Trs.* NIC. DE VALLE (d. 1473) [British Museum, *Early Printed Books*, IV, 13]
Theogonia	1495, Venice (Aldus, with Theocritus) [Hain 15477]	1474, Ferrara (A. Belfortis) *Trs.* BON. MOMBRITIUS (d. 1482) [Hain 8541]
HIEROCLES *In Pythagorae aureos versus Comm.*	1583, Paris (Nivelle)	1474, Padua (Bart. de Valdezoccho) *Trs.* G. AURISPA (before 1455) [Hain 8545]
HOMER *Ilias*	1488–9, Florence (B. de Nerli)	1474, Rome (J. P. de Lignamine) *Trs.* NIC. DE VALLE (d. 1473) (Partial translation of single cantos in verse) 1474, Brescia (H. de Colonia) *Trs.* LOR. VALLA (Books I–XVI) 1444 [Hain 8780] and FRANC. GRIFFOLINI OF AREZZO (d. *c.* 1460) (Books XVII–XXIV) (Prose translation) [Hain 8774]
Odyssea	1488–9, Florence (B. de Nerli)	1510, Rome (Jac. Mazochius) *Trs.* RAPH. VOLATERRANUS (d. 1522) 1510, Strassburg (Jo. Schott) *Trs.* JO. TORTELLIUS (d. 1466)
Batrachomyomachia	1486, Venice (Laonicus) [Hain 8782]	*c.* 1471, Venice (unknown printer) *Trs.* CARLO MARSUPPINI (d. 1453) [Hain 8784; British Museum, *Early Printed Books*, V, 583] 1510, Vienna (Hier Vietor) *Trs.* JO. REUCHLIN (d. 1522) [Denis, *Wiens Buchdruck*, 317] 1512, Deventer (Jac. de Breda) *Trs.* AEDICOLLIUS. SERV. [Nijhoff-Kronenberg 3182] 1513, Wittenberg (Grünenberg) *Trs.* PHILYMNUS (in Greek and Latin)
HORUS APOLLO *Hieroglyphica*	1505, Venice (Aldus, with Aesop)	1517, Bologna (Plato de Benedictis) *Trs.* PHIL. PHASIANINUS 1518, Basle (Froben) *Trs.* BERN. TREBATIUS

AUTHOR AND TITLE	FIRST GREEK PRINTING	LATIN TRANSLATIONS
IAMBLICHUS *De Mysteriis Aegyptiorum*	1678, Oxford U.P.	1497, Venice (Aldus) *Trs.* MARS. FICINUS (d. 1499) [Hain 9358]
ISOCRATES *Orationes*	1493, Milan (Scinzenzeler) [Hain 9312]	
Or. ad Nicoclem de Regno		1480, Venice (P. de Plasiis) *Trs.* FRANC. BUZACARINUS (1479–80) [British Museum, *Early Printed Books*, v, 268] 1492, Venice (B. Benalius, with Giustiniani, *Orationes et Epist.*) *Trs.* BERN. GIUSTINIANI (1408–89) [Hain 9639] 1516, Louvain (Th. Martens, with *Institutio Principis Christiani*) *Trs.* ERASMUS [Nijhoff-Kronenberg 830 and 2952]
Ad Demonicum de Modo Bene Vivendi	1493, Milan (Scinzenzeler) [Hain 9312]	*c.* 1495, Heidelberg (H. Knoblochtzer) *Trs.* R. AGRICOLA (d. 1485) [Hain 9316] *c.* 1495, Nürnberg (F. Creussner) [Hain 9317] 1512, Deventer (Jac. de Breda) [Nijhoff-Kronenberg 3243] 1519, Deventer (A. Pafraet) [Nijhoff-Kronenberg 3244] Also in R. Agricola, *Paraenesis*, 1508 [Nijhoff-Kronenberg 47] Also in R. Agricola, *Opuscula*, 1511, Antwerp (Th. Martens) [Nijhoff-Kronenberg 46] 1518, Louvain (Th. Martens, with Cato, *Disticha*) *Trs.* ERASMUS [Nijhoff-Kronenberg 537] 1515, Strassburg (Jo. Knoblouch) *Trs.* OTHMAR LUSCINIUS [Proctor 10091]
De Laudibus Helenae	1493, Milan (Scinzenzeler) [Hain 9312]	*c.* 1495, Venice (Chr. de Pensis) *Trs.* JOANNES PETRUS LUCENSIS [Hain 9314]
JOANNES CHRYSOSTOMUS	1529, Verona (Sabio, *In Pauli Epistolas*) 1612, Eton (Norton, *Opera omnia*, 8 vols.)	1466, Cologne (Ulr. Zel), *Super Psalmum Miserere* *Trs.* ? [Hain 5032] *c.* 1470, Cologne (Ulr. Zel), *De Patientia in Job* *Trs.* LILIUS TIFERNAS (before 1455) [Hain 5024] (Other Ulr. Zel quartos of single homilies Hain 5048, 5051–2)

AUTHOR AND TITLE	FIRST GREEK PRINTING	LATIN TRANSLATIONS
JOANNES CHRYSOSTOMUS [*cont.*]		n.a. 1466, Strassburg (Jo. Mentelin), *Homiliae super Matthaeum* *Trs.* GEORGIUS TRAPEZUNTIUS (d. 1486) [Hain 5034] 1470, Rome (G. Lauer), *Homiliae super Johannem* *Trs.* FRANC. GRIFFOLINI OF AREZZO (d. 1466) [Hain 5036] 1479, Brussels (Brothers of Common Life), *Homiliae XXI* *Trs.* PETRUS BALBUS, bp. of Tropea (d. 1479) [Hain 5038] *c.* 1470, Rome (G. Lauer), *Homiliae XXV* *Trs.* CHRIST. PERSONA (d. 1486) [Hain 5039]*
JOSEPHUS FLAVIUS *De Antiquitate Judaica*	1544, Basle (Froben & Episcopius)	All Latin eds. from 1470, Augsburg (Schüssler) onwards reprint a late antique Latin version by Rufinus (?) [Hain 9451] *Trs.* There are, as far as I know, no Renaissance translations
LIBANIUS *Opera*	1517, Ferrara (Mazochius)	1504, Cracow (Clymes for Haller) *Trs.* F. ZAMBECCARI (1474)
Epistolae	1499, Venice (Aldus), in *Epistolae Div. Philosophorum*) [Hain 6659]	1519, Louvain (Th. Martens) *Trs.* ERASMUS OF ROTTERDAM, *Aliquot Declamatiunculae* [Nijhoff-Kronenberg 1367]
LUCIAN OF SAMOSATA	1496, Florence (F. de Alopa) [Hain 10258]	1470, Rome (G. Lauer) *Trs.* Five dialogues by BERTHOLDUS, RINUCCIO OF AREZZO, G. AURISPA, CHR. PERSONA [Hain 10269] *c.* 1475, Nürnberg (F. Creussner) *Trs.* F. GRIFFOLINI OF AREZZO, (d. 1460) *Calumnia*, with Diogenes Cynicus, *Epistolae* [Hain 6192] 1475, Naples (A. de Bruxella) *Trs.* LILIUS CASTELLANUS, *Verae Narrationes* [Hain 10259] 1494, Venice (S. Bevilaqua) *Opuscula plurima* (Thirteen Dialogues) adding to the five printed at Rome, 1470, eight others translated by GUARINO DA VERONA, LILIUS CASTELLANUS, POGGIO and others anon. [Hain 10261]

* Etc. Hain 5024–5055 describes thirty-two fifteenth-century Latin editions, most of them not indicating the translators' names. In the sixteenth century Erasmus translated a number of Chrysostom's homilies (see Vanderhaeghen, *Bibl. Erasmiana* (1893), II, 35–6).

AUTHOR AND TITLE	FIRST GREEK PRINTING	LATIN TRANSLATIONS
MAXIMUS TYRIUS Sermones	1557, Paris (H. Stephanus)	1517, Rome (Jac. Mazochius) Trs. COSM. PACCIUS (d. 1513)
MOSCHUS in Amorem Fugitivum	1565, Bruges (Goltzius), ed. Mekerch. (? possibly before that wrongly as 'Theocritus')	Trs. BAPT. GUARINUS (1434–1513) Wrongly as 'Lucian' in Lucian, Opuscula plurima, Venice, Bevilaqua, 1494 and in all reprints of that collection★
NEMESIUS OF EMESA De Natura Hominis	1565, Antwerp (Plantin)	1512, Strassburg (M. Schürer) Trs. JO. CONO, O.P., of Nürnberg. Wrongly published as Gregorii Nyssae episc. libri octo de Homine
ONOSANDER Strategica	1599, Paris (Saugrain)	1494, Rome (E. Silber, with Vegetius) Trs. NIC. SAGUNDINUS [Hain 15915]
OPPIANUS De Piscibus	1515, Florence (Giunta)	1478, Colle di Valdelsa (Bonus Gallus) Trs. LAUR. LIPPI [Hain 12015]
ORIGENES	? 1733–59, Paris, 4 vols., ed. La Rue	1481, Rome (G. Herolt) Trs. CHRIST. PERSONA (d. 1486), Contra Celsum lib. VIII [Hain 12078] 1536, Basle (Froben & Episcopius) Trs. ERASMUS OF ROTTERDAM (d. 1536), Opera lat. studio et labore Erasmi partim versa, partim recognita
ORPHEUS Argonautica	1500, Florence (Giunta)	1519, Bologna, with Valerius Flaccus Trs. LEODRISIUS CRIVELLI (d. 1476)
PAUSANIAS Graeciae Descriptio	1516, Venice (Aldus)	c. 1500, Venice (O. de Luna) Trs. DOM. CALDERINUS (d. 1478) (Attica only), British Museum, Early Printed Books, v, 570 [Hain 12526]
PHALARIS Epistolae	1498, Venice (Pelusius, Bracius, Bissolus and Mangius) [Hain 12871]	c. 1469, Rome (Ulr. Han.) Trs. FRANC. GRIFFOLINI OF AREZZO (d. 1460) [Hain 12874]
PLATO Opera	1513, Venice (Aldus)	1485, Florence (L. de Alopa) Trs. MARSILIUS FICINUS (d. 1499) [Hain 13062] c. 1475, Bologna (anon. press) Trs. LEONARDI BRUNI OF AREZZO, (d. 1444) Gorgias, Apologia Socratis (British Museum, Early Printed Books, VI, 812 note) [Hain 13065]
Epistolae	1499, Venice (Aldus, Epist. Div. Philosoph.) [Hain 6659]	c. 1470, Paris (Gering, Krantz & Friburger) Trs. LEONARDO BRUNI OF AREZZO (d. 1444) [Hain 13066]

★ See L. Bertalot in Miscellanea Mercati IV (1946), p. 321: Antologia di Epigrammi di Lorenzo Abstemio—'dell Amore fugitivo si hanno almeno tre versioni umanistiche del sec. xv.'

AUTHOR AND TITLE	FIRST GREEK PRINTING	LATIN TRANSLATIONS
PLATO [cont.] *Axiochus de Contemnenda* *Morte*		c. 1480, Deventer (R. Paffraet) Trs. RUD. AGRICOLA (d. 1485) [Campbell, *Annales*, 1419]
PLOTINUS *Opera*	1580, Basle (Perna)	1492, Florence (Miscomini) Trs. MARS. FICINUS (d. 1499) [Hain 13121]
PLUTARCH *Vitae Parallelae*	1517, Florence (Giunta)	c. 1470, Rome (Ulr. Han.) ed. J. A. Campanus [Hain 13125] After 1471, Strassburg (A. Rusch) [Hain 13124] 1478, Venice (N. Jenson)★ [Hain 13127]
De Liberis Educandis	1496, Florence (Alopa, in Cebes, *Tabula*) [GW 6442]	c. 1472, Cologne (Terhoernen) [Hain 13146] 1472, Parma (Portilia) [Hain 13147] Trs. GUARINO DA VERONA (d. 1460)
Moralia	1509, Venice (Aldus)	c. 1471, Venice (Printer of Basilius), [Hain 13139] 1471, Venice (Vind. de Spira) [Hain 13140]
[*Apophthegmata*]		c. 1473, Utrecht (Ketelaer & de Leempt) Trs. F. PHILELPHUS (d. 1481) [Campbell, *Annales*, 1423]
[*De Claris Mulieribus*]		1485, Brescia (Bon. de Boninis), and perhaps earlier undated editions? Trs. ALAM. RINUCCINI (?) [Hain 13144]
[*Problemata*]		c. 1476–7, Venice (Dom. de Siliprandis) Trs. JO. PETRUS LUCENSIS [Hain 13137]
[*De Brevibus cl. Virorum* *Contentionibus*] [*De Tranquillitate Animi* *De Fortuna Romanorum* *De Virtute Alexandri*]		1485, Brescia (Bon. de Boninis) Trs. JO. LAVAGNOLUS [Hain 13150] 1505, Paris (Jod. Badius) Trs. GUIL. BUDÉ [Ph. Renouard, Badius, III, 171–2]

★ These three early editions are printed after different MSS., for although they all profess to indicate the translators of each of the Lives, they diverge considerably in their attributions. Thus the first of the Lives, Theseus, is given to Philelphus in the Rome edition, to 'Lapus' (i.e. Lapo di Castiglionchio jr.) in the Strassburg edition; and so on. The *British Museum Cat. of Early Printed Books*, IV, p. 21 tells us nothing at all on the translators. But the (older) General Catalogue has this summary: 'Translated by F. Filelfo, G. Tortelli, Lapo Birago, D. Acciaiuoli, Guarino Veron, Ant. Pasini Tudertinus, F. Barbaro, Leon. B. Aretino, L. Giustiniano.' There is obviously still a good deal of investigation to be undertaken for anyone wishing to establish the identity of each translation as printed in these three editions. But it would be a laborious task.

AUTHOR AND TITLE	FIRST GREEK PRINTING	LATIN TRANSLATIONS
PLUTARCH [*cont.*]		
[*De Placitis Philosophorum*]		1506, Paris (Jod. Badius) [Ph. Renouard, Badius, III, 172]*
POLYBIUS *Historiae*	1530, Hagenau (Secerius)	1472, Rome (Sweynheim & Pannartz) *Trs.* NIC. PEROTTUS (d. 1480) [Hain 13246]
PROCLUS *De Sphaera*	1499, Venice (Aldus, in *Astronomici Veteres* [Hain 14559]	*Trs.* THOMAS LINACRE (d. 1524) in the same vol. as Greek
PROCOPIUS *Historiae*	1607, Augsburg	1506, Rome (Jac. Mazochius), *De Bello Gothorum* 1509, Rome (E. Silber), *De Bello Persico Trs.* CHR. PERSONA (d. 1486)
PTOLEMY		
Almagest	1538, Basle (Walderus)	1528, Venice (Giunta) *Trs.* GEORGE OF TREBIZOND (1399–1486)†
Geographia	1533, Basle (Froben & Episcopius)	1475, Vicenza (H. Liechtenstein) *Trs.* JAC. ANGELI DE SCARPARIA (1410) [Hain 13536]
PYTHAGORAS *Aurei Versus*	1495, Venice (Aldus, Lascaris, *Erotemata*) [Hain 9924]	1474, Padua. See Hierocles above *Trs.* G. AURISPA (d. 1459)§
STRABO *Geographia*	1516, Venice (Aldus)	1469, Rome (Sweynheim & Pannartz) *Trs.* GUARINO DA VERONA (d. 1460) & GREGORIUS TIFERNAS (d. 1466) [Hain 15086]
SYNESIUS *De Laudibus Calvitii*	1553, Paris (A. Turnebus, in (?) *Opuscula*)	1515, Basle (Froben), with Erasmus, *Moriae Encomium Trs.* JO. PHREA (Free) (d. 1465)
THEOCRITUS *Idyllia*	*c.* 1481, Milan (B. Accursius) [Hain 15476]	1510, Paris (J. Petit) (hardly the first edition) *Trs.* MARINUS PHILETICUS, poet laureate *c.* 1420
THEOPHRASTUS *Historia Plantarum*	1497, Venice (Aldus, in Aristotle, *Opera*) [GW 2334, vol. IV]	1483, Treviso (B. de Confaloneriis) *Trs.* THEOD. GAZA (d. 1478) [Hain 15491]

* To extend this enumeration beyond 1509, the date of the first Greek printed edition, would render it far too voluminous.

† Joh. Regiomontanus announced the impending publication of his own Latin version in his broadside of 1474 (Hain 13807), but it never appeared and it is doubtful if it ever got to a printable stage. He certainly had owned the Greek MS. from which the Editio Princeps was printed.

§ I doubt if there are earlier Latin impressions of Aurispa's translation, though there are a great number of reprints in various composite publications and alone.

AUTHOR AND TITLE	FIRST GREEK PRINTING	LATIN TRANSLATIONS
THEOPHRASTUS *Characteres*	1527, Nürnberg (Petreius, ed. Bil. Pirckheymer)	1531, Basle (Cratander) *Trs.* ANG. POLIZIANO (d. 1494) 1527, Nürnberg (printed with the Greek) *Trs.* BIL. PIRCKHEYMER (d. 1530)
THEOPHYLACTUS (Archiep. Bulgariae eleventh century) *Commentarii in d. Pauli Epistolas*	1636, London, e Typographeo Regio	1477, Rome (Ulr. Han.) *Trs.* CHRIST. PERSONA (d. 1486) under the title, *Athanasius in epistolas S. Pauli* [Hain 1902]
THUCYDIDES *De Bello Peloponnesiaco*	1502, Venice (Aldus)	1483, Treviso (Jo. Rubeus) *Trs.* L. VALLA (d. 1457) [Hain 15511]
XENOPHON *Opera*	1516, Florence (Giunta)	*c.* 1500, Milan (Guil. Le Signerre) *Trs.* OMNIBONUS LEONICENUS, PHILELPHUS, LEON. BRUNI OF AREZZO [Hain 16225]
Cyropaedia		1477, Milan (Ungardus) *Trs.* F. PHILELPHUS, 1467 [Hain 16227]
Memorabilia		1521, Rome (Mazochius) *Trs.* BESSARION (d. 1472)

APPENDIX C

TYPE FACSIMILES

FIGURE I

DOCTISSIMI VIRI HENRICI
Bulloci theologiæ doctori ⸱, oratio habita Cā
tabrigiæ, in frequentiſſimo cetu, præ
ſentibus Cæſaris oratoribus,
& nonnullis alŋs epiſco
pis, ad reueren⸗
diſs. D.
Tho
mā Car⸗
dinalem titulo
ſanctæ Ceciliæ, Lega⸗
tum a latere, Archiepiſcopum
Eboracenſem,& Angliæ ſupremum
Cancellarium.

Apud præclariſſimam academiam Canta⸗
brigienſem. An. M.quingenteſimouiceſi⸗
moprimo.

Bullock, *Oratio*, 1521. The first book Siberch printed
in Cambridge. (See pp. 2–4.)

FIGURE 2

Sententiæ aliquot, Græcæ
& Latinæ.

Fidos amicos fratres exiftimare debes.
νόμιζ᾽ ἀδελφοὺς τοὺς ἀλκίνους φίλους.
Nõ eft inuenire uitã abſꝗ moleſtia ullã,
ὀυκ ἔsιν ἐυϱεῖν βίον ἄλυπον ὀυδενί,
Deo certe nullus fortunatus hoĩm fine
θεοῦ γαὴ ὀυδεὶς ἐυτυχεῖν βϱοτῶν ἄνευ
Malis conuerſans & ipſe euades malus.
κακοῖς ὁμιλῶν κἀυτὸϱ᾽ ἐκβίση κακός.

Impreſſum eft hoc opuſcülum Can‑
tabrigiæ, per Ioannem Siberch,
Anno, M. D. XXI.

Lucian, *Dipsades*, printed by Siberch, Cambridge, 1521.
This is the first appearance of any Greek type in England.
The Latin translation is by Bullock. (See p. 4.)

FIGURE 3

tiſſime de te, ac ſtudio tuo ꝙ optimam & certiſſimam
ſpem habere, Tui muneris omnino iam eſſe videtur
Alexander, vt plane efficias, ne me falſo hæc dixiſſe
arbitretur, & ne hac ſpe, in quam ego illum, mea con／
ſtantiſſima predicatione erexſ, demū fruſtratus eſſe
videaꝼ, Quod vt ſedulo: diligenter: & accurate facias
non ſolum te moneo, ſed & hortor, vrgeo, impello,
Interim vero Hos Luciani Dialogos iucundiſſimos
& vtiliſſimos (Sunt aūt Scipio: Scaphidiū: palinur⁹
virt⁹ et Hercules) ꝗs ꝑuati tibi dedicatoſ, ī vſum publí
cum edo, diligenter lege, illis veluti cum quibuſdam
amantiſſimis conuictoribus te oblecta creberrime,
Non olei: crede mihi: nec opere te penitebit, ita aures
tuas teneras adhuc, & molliculas ſuauiſſimo quodā
ſermonis ſono implebunt, & ora certo obtutu defixa
Soloꝗ intentos oculos: vt es maiuſcularū rerum mi
rator egregius: aliquandiu tenebunt, Qua re autem
tenebunt? Nempe rerum gratiſſima varietate: voca
bulorum ſplendore nitidiſſimo: ſententiarum grauiſ
ſimo pondere: ac totius fere lacialis eloquij expreſſa
facie, Sed vt mea Epiſtola ſuum aliquando penſum
abſoluat, Iam Vale, & bonis litteris acriter incumbe,
Ego preceptor, ac monitor, tuis in hac redeſyderijs
nunꝗ deero, Age tu modo, ne tib iipſi defuiſſe videa／
ris, Iterū Vale, & ſalue, Lipſi, octauo Kalendas Dece／
bres. Anno natalis Chriſtiani Milleſimo quingente／
ſimodecimotertio,

Epistola Obscurorum Virorum. Printed by Heinrich Gran, Hagenau,
Alsace. The first edition, 1515. (See pp. 36–7.)

86

FIGURE 4

augurium:hic gallina ſyluatica. Inde ornitheras
auceps. Ornithia græce ορνιθεια ludi in quo pu/
eri uerberabātur : tempus quod eſt ſeptuageſimo
die poſt brumam quando aues adueniunt ut hyrū
dines ciconiæ Ornitoboſcion:loc⁹ ad alēdas gal
linas & aues. Bactra regio:pluriphariis diuitis ut
Quintus Curtius ait referta:nominitata ab Oboc
tro āneInde bactrius a.um.& Bactriani populi ipſi
Lupus:piſcis græce λαβραξ hunc opici & barbari
Lucium:Picentes uarulum uocant.
Muſtellæ:piſces in lacu brigantino Retie murenis
fere ſimiles quas a lambendis petris uuſgo nunc
lampetras uocāt.   Gammarus genus cancri:
quod a carabis:paguris:aſtacis :meis: heraclcoti/
cis:leonibus:ac hippis ſpecie differt.
Sthenelus:cygnus:holor.   τελοσ

Eiuſdē Georgii Diſtichō ad Petrū Erythrapolitanū
Accipe iam pingui gloſſemata noſtra Minerua :
    Poſt hac ſi uiuam mox meliora dabo

Expreſſum Erphordie per Enricum Sertoriū
Blancopolitanum Anno domini milleſimo
quingenteſimo primoad calendas octobres

Hesiod, printed at Marschalk's Erfurt press by
Sertorius, 1501. (See p. 42.)

FIGURE 5

SECVNDVS

Infiuuare ratem ius fecerat exulit oris
Omnibus externas ueheret per inhofpita gazas
Aequora & infano penderet fæpe profundo
Omnia fed cunctis nafci dabat aurea terris
Iufticia :& nullo difcreuerat aere regna.
At poftquā argento deformis uiluit ætas
Rarius in terras os inclinabat honeftum
Iam dea uix fummos adlabens deniq; montis
Concedente die Phœbus fub nocte propinqua
Occiduus prono furgeret in equora currus
Vfurpandam oculis fe dabat ad currentum
Non ut feffa uirum repararet gaudia uultu
Sed crepula ut late uomeret cōuicia uocẹ
Parcite uile genus lachrymis aiebat ab ortis
Caufa querelarū ueftrū eft fcelus aurea quondā
Iudice me ueftri uixerunt fæcla parentes
Degener in uobis animus :folertia uobis
Per uigil :arte noua uitam traducere mos eft.
Omne euū ftudiis excuditis hinc quoq; rurfum
Proh pudor atq; dolor nafcetur uilior ætas
Et lacerata genas ibit bellona per urbes
Saucia ut infidas agitent certamina metas.
Hec ubi per mefto rauco congefferat ore
Alter pro curfu fefe in conuexa ferebat
Protinus atq; oculos fugiens exofa fequentū
Linquebat cetus hominū ruit:hæc quoq; rurfum
Viuendi feries ac fucceffere pudendo

a iii

Marschalk, *Oratio Albiori Habita*, printed at his Wittenberg
press by Trebelius, 1503. (See p. 42.)

FIGURE 6

SCAPHIDIVM,

nus eſſe potuerim, moriēs quattuor & viginti ſolū li-
bras argēti reliquerim, Illud nō tacebo: ſcilicet me nū-
q̃ iniuſtū, aut crudelē fuiſſe, aut alicuius generis volu
ptate corruptū, Et hęc vt in principio dixi nō ea rōne
q̃ preferri velīm retuli: ſed graue erat non monſtrare:
vt eſt: romanos omni genere virtutū cæteras gentes
ſuperaſſe, Itacꝗ vt viuus ꝓ patria pugnaui, patriæcꝗ
pietatē mihi & rebus cæteris prætuli: ſic nūc apud te
o Minos ꝓ patria hęc dicta ſunt, MI, per Iouem o Sci
pio, & recte, & vti romanum decet loquutus es. Itacꝗ
diſciplina militari, rebuſcꝗ bellicis hiſce æqualem aut
te pſtantiorē ſciamus te præferendū cenſeo, & Alexā
der ſecundus ſit, & tertius Hannibal, nec hic quidem
ſpernendus eſt,

LVCIANI SCAPHIDIVM LOCVTO
RES, CHARON, MERCVRIVS, MENI
PPVS, CARMOLAVS, LAMPICIVS,
DAMASIAS, CRATON, MICO, PHI-
LOSOPHVS, CHARON,

Vdite quo quidem pacto noſtra ſe nego
a   tia habeant: parua em̄ (vt videtis) ac vet⁹
nobis eſt nauicula: rimiſcꝗ fatiſcit, ac fluctuū impul-
ſione naufraga eſt, Vos vero nonnulli ſimul adueni-

B

Lucian, *Dialogues*, printed by Melchior Lotter, Leipzig, 1513.
(See p. 44.)

89

FIGURE 7

GREGORII, COELLII, AVBANI, IN TABEL-
LAS. R. CROCI, PRECEPTORIS SVI,
EPIGRAMMA EXTEMPO-
RARIVM.

Si cui : nec docti Gazæ : nec Lafcharis vnç̃

    Terfa nec vrbani fcripta videre datum eft,

Nec veteres , graij ftudij: linguæcp parentes,

    Grammaticos, doctis nomina nota viris:

Ille mei (moneo) Richardi fcripta magiftri

    Et legat. & paruo in codice cuncta legat

IN TABELLAS.

Vidit vt has pallas confcriptas forte tabellas :

    Mirata ingenium docte Ricarde tuum:

βάλλ ούτωσ dixit, grece fpes maxima lingue.

    Et pitura mihi viuere regna iube.

Nancp potes.nec em flenda eft mihi grecia: Marte

    Dum Germana tuo regna parata manent

ταῦτα ὁρῶσα κρόκον Δαιδάλεα σχήματ᾽ ἀθήνη

  ούποτ ἀθηναίων σκῆπτρα ἀπώλεσ ἔφη

ἀλλ ἅμα γερμάνων τε ἀρχιφίλων τε βρεταρμῶν

  πολλὰ κρατῶ.τῶν πρίν μηδὲν ἔλαττον ἔχω

Croke, *Tabulae graecas literas*, printed by Valentin Schumann,
Leipzig, 1516. (See pp. 38, 44.)

FIGURE 8

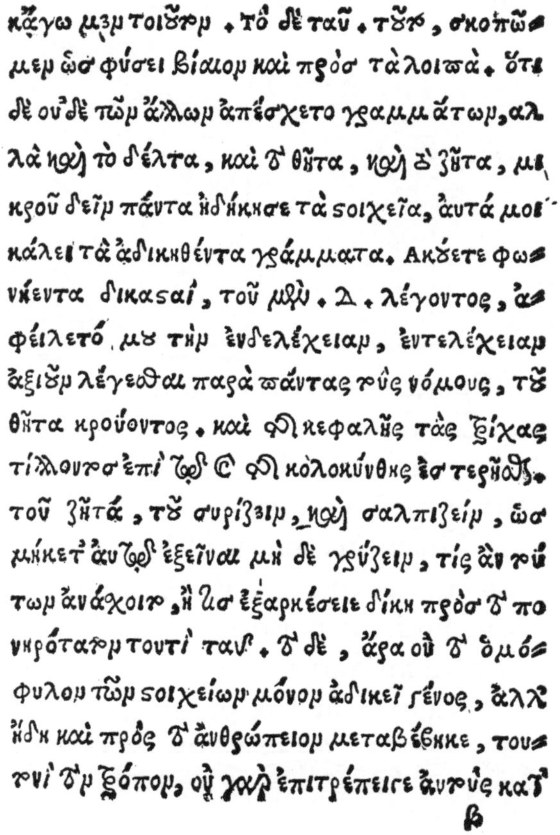

κἀγὼ μὲν τοιȣ̃τον , τὸ δὲ ταῦ , τȣ̃τ , σκοπῶσ
μεν ὡσ φύσει βίαιον καὶ πρόσ τὰ λοιπὰ . ὅτι
δὲ οὐδὲ τῶν ἄλλων ἀπέσχετο γραμμάτων, αλ
λὰ καὶ τὸ δέλτα , καὶ δ᾽ θῆτα , καὶ ζ̃ ζῆτα , μι
κροῦ δεῖν πάντα ἠδίκησε τὰ soιχεῖα , αὐτά μοι
κάλει τὰ ἀδικηθέντα γράμματα. Ακȣετε φω
νήεντα δικαsαί , τοῦ μȣ̃ . Δ . λέγοντος , ἀ
φείλετό μȣ τὴν ἐνδελέχειαν , ἐντελέχειαν
ἀξιȣ̃ν λέγεϑαι παρὰ πάντας ρὺσ νόμους , τȣ̃
θῆτα κροȣ́οντος . καὶ ϕ κεφαλῆσ τὰσ τρίχασ
τίλλουσ᾽ ἐπὶ ϖ ΄ ϕ κολοκύνθης ἐσ τερῆϑ̃.
τοῦ ζῆτα , τȣ̃ συρίζειν , καὶ σαλπιζείν , ὡσ
μήκετ᾽ αὐτȣ̃ ἐξεῖναι μὴ δὲ γρύζειν , τίσ ἂν τȣ̃
των ἀνάχοιν , ἢ ἲσ ἐξαρκέσειε δίκη πρόσ δ᾽ πο
νηρότατȣν τουτί ταῦ . δ᾽ δὲ , ἄρα οὐ δ᾽ ὁμό
φυλον τῶν soιχείων μόνον ἀδικεῖ γένος , ἀλλ᾽
ἤδη καὶ πρὸσ δ᾽ ἀνθρώπειον μεταβέϐηκε , τουσ
ρυῒ δ᾽ν τρόπον, οὐ γαρ̀ ἐπιτρέπεισ αὐτȣ̃σ κατ᾽
β

Lucian, *Iuditium Vocalium*, printed by
Schumann, Leipzig, 1523.

FIGURE 9

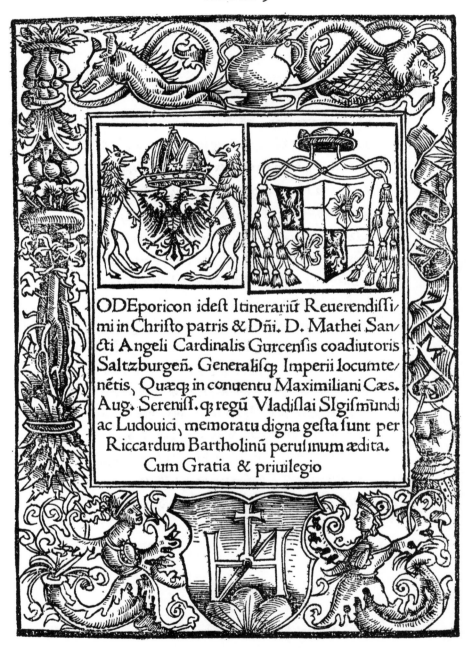

Bartholinus, *Odeporicon*—'The Vienna Meeting of Kings'—
printed by Vietor, Vienna, 1515. (See p. 45.)

κατιόντεσ, ἄρτι μὲν ταῦροι, ἄρτι δὲ σάτυροι καὶ
κύκνοι γενόμενοι καὶ θεοὺσ ἐξ αὐτῶν ποιεῖσθαι ἀξιοῦν
τεσ. ἀλλ' ἐχρῆν ἴσωσ φήσεισ ἀναπεπλάσθαι τοὺσ
ἀνθρώπουσ ἄλλον τινα τρόπον ἀλλὰ μὴ ἡμῖν ἐρι
κότασ καὶ τί ἄλλο παράδειγμα τούτου ἄμεινον
προεστὺσ ἄμιν ὃ πάντωσ καλὸν ἠπιστάμιν, ἢ ἄσι
νετον καὶ θηριῶδεσ ἔδει καὶ ἄγριον ἀπεργάζεσθαι
τὸ ζῶον, καὶ πῶσ ἂν ἢ θεοῖσ εὔσαν ἢ τὰσ ἄλλασ
ὑμῖν τιμᾶσ ἀπενειμᾶν οὐχὶ τοιοῦτοι γενόμενοι.
ἀλλ' ὑμεῖσ ὅταν μὲν ὑμῖν τὰσ ἑκατόμβασ προ=
σάγωσιν οὐκ ὀκνεῖτε κἂν ἐπὶ τὸν ὠκεανὸν ἐλθεῖν
δέοι μετ' ἀμύμονασ αἰθιοπῆασ τὸν δὲ τῶν τιμῶν
ὑμῖν καὶ τῶν θυσιῶν αἴτιον ἀνεσταυρώκατε. περὶ
μὲν οὖν τῶν ἀνθρώπων, καὶ ταῦτα ἱκανά, ἤδη δὲ
εἰ δοκεῖ ἐπὶ τὸ πῦρ μέτειμι, καὶ τὴν ἐπονείδιστον
ταύτην κλοπὴν, καὶ πρὸσ θεῶν τοῦτό μοι ἀπόκρι
ναι μηδὲν ὀκνήσασ ἐσθ' ὅτι ἡμεῖσ τοῦ πυρόσ ἀπολω
λέκαμεν ἐξ ὅτου καὶ παρ' ἀνθρώποισ ἐστίν, οὐκ ἂν
εἴποισ, αὐτη γὰρ οἶμαι φύσισ τουτουὶ τοῦ κτήμα=
τοσ, οὐδὲν τι ἔλαττον γίγνεται εἰ καί τισ ἄλλοσ
αὐτοῦ μεταλάβοι, οὐ γὰρ ἀποσβέννυται ἐναυσα=
μένου τινόσ, φθόνοσ δὴ ἄντικρυσ τὸ τοιοῦτο, ἀφ'

π.ι.

Lucian, printed by Gilles de Gourmont, Paris, 1509–10.
(See pp. 49–50.)

FIGURE II

MORIAE ENCOMI VM ERA SMI ROTERODAMI DECLAMATIO.

Ad Lectorem

Habes hic Lector ἐγκώμιον τῆσ μωρίασ,hoc eſt laue
dem ſtulticiæ,libellū oppido ᵹ̄ facetiſſimū,ab
Eraſmo Roterodamo Germanoᵹ̄ deco
re concinnatū,in quo varij homi
nū ſtatus mire taxant̃.Hunc
tu ſi emeris,& legeris,
diſpereā ſi nō impē
dio gaudebis.
Vale.

Erasmus, *Praise of Folly*, printed by Gilles de Gourmont,
Paris, 1511. (See p. 51.)

INDEX

NOTE. The material in Appendix B is not entered in this Index

Frankfurt on the Oder, printing at, 43

Free, John, 31

Froben, 15, 55–6, 60
portrait by Holbein, Plate II
publishes work by Erasmus, 5, 9, 10–11, 27, 56; by Richard Pace, 17

Gaguin, 47, 49

Galen, *De Temperamentis*, translated by Linacre, 12–14
Methodus Medendi, 71
works in Greek, editio princeps by Aldine Press, 31

Gaza, Theodorus, 53, 71

Geminus, Papyrius, 17–18

Geoffrey of Monmouth, 49

George of Trebizond, 24

Gesta Francorum, 49

Gillis, Peter, of Antwerp, 34

Giustiniani, Bernardo, 26

Glareanus, 36

Gourmont, Gilles de, 1, 49–51, 52, 53, 57, 66, 94; Greek type, 93

Gran, Heinrich, at Hagenau, false imprint, 36

Greek studies, at Bologna, 20, 22
at Cambridge, 1–2, 4–5, 21, 31, 38–9
at Cologne, 35–6
in England, 31–2, 63
at Leipzig, 1, 36–8
at Louvain, 34–5
at Paris, 47, 49
at Rome, 29
in Spain, 30–1
in Western Europe, 21–40

Greek texts, Latin translations of, 4, 12–13, 22–8

Greek type, accents and breathings, 36–7, 50
at Bologna, 20
earliest cut in Germany, 41
first appearance in England, 4, 21, 61, 85
press established at Rome, 29, 47
used by Froben, 56; by Gilles de Gourmont, 49–50, 93; by Siberch, 2

Gregory of Tours, St, 49

Griffolini, Francesco, of Arezzo, 26, 62

Grocyn, William, 1, 23, 34, 57

Grosseteste, Robert, 31

Guarino da Verona, 21, 22, 25, 26, 27

Guillaume de Conches, *Dogma Moralium Philosophorum*, 49

Guillen de Brocar, Arnao, printer at Alcala, 30

Hagenau in Alsace, 36, 55, 64

Han, Ulrich, printer at Rome, 26

Hebrew books, destruction at Leipzig, 36, 54, 63

Hebrew teaching, 29–30

Hebrew types, 54

Hectoris, Bened., printer at Bologna, 20

Henricus de Harlem, printer at Siena, 20

Henry VII, 46

Henry VIII, 4, 12, 16–17, 27, 32

Hermathena, 16–18, 39, 57, 61

Hermonymus, Georgius, 47

Herodotus, translation by Lorenzo Valla, 24

Hesiod, *Laus Musarum ex Theogonia*, 42, 87
Works and Days, 50

Heynes, Simon, President of Queens', 69, 70

Heynlin, John, of Stein, 3

Holbein, Hans, Froben's artistic assistant, 56
his portrait of Froben, Plate II

Holonius, 6, 59

Homer, 29, 50, 51, 54, 70, 71

Hoogstraeten, Jacobus van, 36

Horace, 44

Horae, Greek, 53

Hoys, Jacques, bookseller at Orléans, 52

Humanists, as patrons of printing, 3–4
and Greek studies, 21–40
their influence on vernacular prose-style, 40

Humphrey, Duke, of Gloucester, 24

Hutten, Ulrich von, 37, 63, 64

Irenicus, F., *Germaniae Exegeseos volumina XII*, 70

Isocrates, 25–6, 54

Jamer de Hanau, Johannes, printer at Frankfurt, 43, 65

Jenson, printer at Venice, 27

Jerome, St, edition by Erasmus, 56, 69, 70

John of Westphalia, printer at Louvain, 53

Juvenal, 53

Kaetz, Peter, letter to Siberch, 1, 57

Kallierges, Zachary, 29

Ketelaer and De Leempt, printers at Utrecht, 27

Keysere, Robert de, printer at Paris, 52, 67

Kyrfoth, Charles, 61

Laer, John of Siegburg, *see* Siberch, John

Lapo de Castiglionchio, the younger, 27

Lascaris, Janus, 29, 53

INDEX

For EU product safety concerns, contact us at Calle de José Abascal, 56–1°,
28003 Madrid, Spain or eugpsr@cambridge.org.

www.ingramcontent.com/pod-product-compliance
Ingram Content Group UK Ltd.
Pitfield, Milton Keynes, MK11 3LW, UK
UKHW030902150625
459647UK00021B/2656